Calling All Angels

ЧИДО ГЕОРГИЯ О ЗМИЕ

Discussions with Dr. Robert W.P. Cutler, M.D. on the Murder of Jane Stanford

STEPHEN HERRICK REQUA
Author of *Great American Gold Grab*

Published by:
Trine Day LLC
PO Box 577
Walterville, OR 97489
1-800-556-2012
www.TrineDay.com
publisher@TrineDay.net

Library of Congress Control Number: 2016947257

Requa, Stephen Herrick.
 – 1st ed.
p. cm.
Includes references and index.
Epub (ISBN-13) 978-1-63424-035-2
Mobi (ISBN-13) 978-1-63424-036-9
Print (ISBN-13) 978-1-63424-034-5
1. Stanford University -- History. 2. Stanford, Jane Lathrop, -- 1828-1905. 3. Murder -- Hawaii -- Honolulu -- History -- Case studies. Requa, Issac L., -- 1828-1905. 4. Gold Mining -- Requa/Hoover Files. I. Requa, Stephen Herrick. II. Title

FIRST EDITION
10 9 8 7 6 5 4 3 2 1

Printed in the USA
Distribution to the Trade by:
Independent Publishers Group (IPG)
814 North Franklin Street
Chicago, Illinois 60610
312.337.0747
www.ipgbook.com

Publisher's Foreword

O, it is excellent
To have a giant's strength,
But it is tyrannous
To use it like a giant.
                    -Isabella, *Measure for Measure*

To suckle fools and chronicle small beer.
                                    – Iago, *Othello*

Power lacks moral or principles. It only has interests.
                            – Horacio Castellanos Moya

What a hell we should make of the world if we could do what we would!
                            – Ralph Waldo Emerson

Stephen Requa, because of fate and history had "things" that the "powers-that-be" wanted ... making his life a holy hell. Matter-of-fact "they" murdered his great grandfather because of things that they wanted ... "to control."

When first confronted with corruption primarily we chalk it up to greed, apathy, or other basic human foibles. But the more you look under the rug, around corners and behind curtains, one finds a concerted, directed effort that goes beyond the basic seven deadly sins and leads to institutionalized evil: The subjugation of human beings by other human beings through deceit, technology, and flimflam using many techniques that are abhorrently inhumane.

It is criminal.

This activity doesn't happen in a vacuum, the collateral damage is all of us: our future, our lives, our children and theirs, our heritage, our country ... our world.

Stephen had his life rudely interrupted, while working in the family's main business – mining. The U.S. shift from a gold-backed currency to Saudi-American petrodollars commenced a consolidation of interests and intrigue. The Requa family had been in mining for generations, Stephen's great-grandfather, Isaac L. Requa made two fortunes in gold, one in California and another in Nevada. He was the president of the Central Pacific Railroad for many years, and related by marriage to Jane Stanford. Isaac's son and Stephen's grandfather, Mark, worked with Stanford alumnus, President Herbert Hoover in collecting the most detailed information on mining, especially gold mining, in the Americas.

The Requa/Hoover files detailed thousands of gold properties from Alaska to Bolivia; the files contained the most plentiful untapped geological data available anywhere for use in finding new gold mines in the U.S. and Central America. These files comprised an enormous body of data that the Requa family had acquired through 150 years of historic gold-mining developments. The Requa/Hoover Files comprised the most complete information available on American gold prospects and deposits.

Gee, wonder why anyone would want that? The shenanigans, death-threats, etc. that followed are chronicled in Requa's book, *The Great American Gold Grab*. Stephen became the unwilling victim of his birth and occupation, for he had continued the family tradition, as had his father, and continued to expand the fortuitous files. And as Dr. William Pepper wrote in the foreword to that book:

> In the annals of history, the classic David-and-Goliath encounter has been many times duplicated. Almost every culture passes down to its children inspiring tales of the courage of a single individual who achieved an unlikely victory over much more powerful opponents. Such heroes have gone against the tide of popular opinion or the interests of the powerful of their time, in the furtherance of principle, simple justice – or just the truth. And almost without exception, those undertaking such efforts have paid a price.

Here in *Calling All Angels*, we learn how and *why* the ultimate price paid by Jane Stanford was covered up … by *upstanding* citizens.

Power and control, because they could and they wanted to – the action advanced their interests. The killing of Jane Stanford and her relation Isaac Requa left Stanford University defenseless – to be used and abused, as it's new owners saw fit. These were turbulent times with change in the air, and as history moved on, the influence of Stanford has been mighty.

My good friend, Professor Antony Sutton, while working at the Hoover Institute at Stanford University, ran directly into the "powers-that-be." They said, "Tony, don't break your rice bowl." Tony became a David.

So has Stephen.

Onwards to the Utmost of Futures!

Peace,

Kris Millegan
Publisher
TrineDay
July 4, 2016

In Memoriam

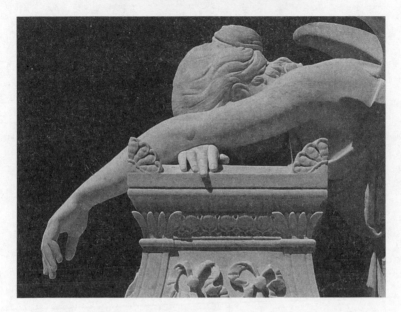

STANFORD MAUSOLEUM – ANGEL OF GRIEF

CALLING ALL ANGELS

Calling all Angels to show me the way
To give me peace in the decisions,
To give me hope in a heaven where we will all be together again,
To give me faith in a God who knows better than me,
The reason for such despair here on earth.

Selection of Prayer by Jane Stanford

Contents

Jane Lathrop Stanford (1828-1905) was a co-founder of Stanford University in 1885 along with her husband, Leland Stanford, as a memorial to their only child, Leland Stanford Jr., who died in 1884 at the age of 15.

Foreword

The Passion of Jane Stanford

As established by Dr. Robert W.P. Cutler, M.D., author of *The Mysterious Death of Jane Stanford* (Stanford Press 2003), the following are details surrounding the death of Jane Stanford on February 28th, 1905.

Not inappropriately, the time from January 14, 1905 to her death may be thought of as "the Passion" of Jane Stanford. It began on the evening of the 14th with her ingesting the contents of bottled water while preparing for bed at her San Francisco mansion. The extremely bitter taste of the water, confirmed by her household help, resulted in an emetic and forced vomiting. An analysis of the bottled water confirmed the presence of strychnine. A detective agency was retained and they sealed off the mansion. On the 15th, Mrs. Stanford wrote to fellow Standford University trustee George Crothers expressing her horror that someone had tried to kill her. Then, accompanied by her secretary Bertha Berner and a maid, she sailed for Honolulu; but, it appears she did not go far enough…

* * * * *

On the evening of the 28th at the Moana Hotel after imbibing bicarbonate of soda, she cried out that she had been poisoned again. Physicians were summoned, in whose immediate presence she succumbed from symptoms diagnostic of strychnine poisoning. Her last words were: "I have been poisoned again. This is a terrible death to die." It was reported on March 1 that "the features of her postural abnormalities, liquid and cyanotic blood, and meningeal inflammation were typical findings of strychnine poisoning. Toxicological analysis revealed strychnine in her intestinal contents and in the bicarbonate of soda." Because of inhomogeneity of the poison in the soda, it was not possible to determine the dose she ingested.

On March 6-9, a coroner's inquest was held at the Moana Hotel. The jury heard the testimony of Mrs Stanford's secretary Bertha Berner, her maid May Hunt, the three physicians, Drs. Humphris, Day and Murray, who were involved in trying to save her, Drs. Shorey and Duncan, who performed the toxicological analyses and Dr Wood, who conducted the autopsy. Based on all the medical and toxicological evidence, on March 9 the official Hawaii State Inquest and Coroner's Jury officially ruled murder by strychnine poisoning "by persons unknown."

Stanford President David Starr Jordan arrived in Honolulu on March 10, accompanied by trustee Timothy Hopkins, Detective Reynolds of the San Francisco Police Department, and Captain Jules Callundan of the Morse Detective Agency that had been retained in the prior poisoning. Their purported purpose was to conduct an "independent investigation" into the cause of Mrs. Stanford's death and then accompany her body to Palo Alto.

On March 15, Jordan drafted a statement for the press that said:

> In our judgment, after careful consideration of all facts brought to our knowledge, we are fully convinced that Mrs. Stanford's death was not due to strychnine poisoning nor to intentional wrong-doing on the part of any one. We find in the statements of those with her in her last moments, no evidence that any of the characteristic symptoms of strychnine poisoning were present. We think it probable that her death was due to a combination of conditions and circumstances. Among these we may note, in connection with her advanced age, the unaccustomed exertion, a surfeit of unsuitable food and the unusual exposure on the picnic party of the day in question.... The occurrence of the strychnine in the bicarbonate of soda is as yet unexplained. The fact that it is not in excess of usual medicinal proportions suggests either an error of a pharmacist or else that the combination was prepared for tonic purposes.

He instructed Stanford alumnus, Judge Carl Smith, to release the statement after his party had set sail back to San Francisco. He also instructed Smith to release a statement to the Associated Press that Miss Berner had taken the same dose of bicarbonate as Mrs.

Stanford and had suffered no ill effects. This "fabricated story," as referred to by Dr. Cutler, was later retracted.

Finally, in an interview with a reporter, Jordan stated that Mrs. Stanford's primary attending physician at the time of her death, Dr. F. Howard Humphris, who lived at the Moana Hotel where Mrs. Stanford was staying, and the other physicians involved *"knew nothing about strychnine poisoning"* and were "deficient in the scientific side." On March 17, the three physicians involved in Mrs. Stanford's case issued a rebuttal of Jordan's conclusions, saying "no Board of Health would accept Jordan's diagnosis as correct."

Back at Stanford, on March 21, Jordan wrote Board President Samuel Leib to say that "if a tonic theory of the strychnine/bicarbonate mixture is not acceptable, the alternative for their use was that Humphris had put the strychnine in the soda after Mrs. Stanford's death. Having made a diagnosis of poisoning, he laced the soda with strychnine to bolster his diagnosis." Jordan described Dr. Humphris as "a man of no personal or professional reputation."

On May 26, Jordan's Stanford officials issued a statement that a re-examination of Mrs. Stanford's organs in university laboratories revealed no evidence of poison, upholding Jordan's conviction of death by natural causes.

Immediately after the Honolulu autopsy, however, all of the organs (apart from the brain and heart which were fixed in formaldehyde) had been turned over to the Hawaiian chemists for analysis. They had been chopped, boiled and reduced to a slurry so the strychnine could be extracted. All that remained of them had been poured down the mortuary drain. *They no longer existed.* Their purported 're-examination' was only possible as pure fiction.

On August 23, 1905, a Honolulu newspaper reported that trustee Timothy Hopkins who had accompanied Jordan to Honolulu had tried to bribe the Honolulu physicians to drop the diagnosis of strychnine poisoning.

The Mysterious Death of Jane Stanford by Robert W.P. Cutler, M.D. was published in July, 2003, and shows that Jane Stanford was poisoned and her murder was covered up.

Calling All Angels

O n July 29, 2001, while in London, I received a quite un-
expected email from a retired Stanford Medical School
neurologist and former Dean of Faculty, Dr. Robert W.P.
Cutler, M.D. He had located a Stanford University internal administration memorandum written about a meeting I attended in
1983 in Hawaii, where researcher and historian Robert Van Dyke
imparted to me his purported discoveries about the 1905 poisoning death of Jane Stanford.

On a visit to Stanford later in 1983, I had mentioned my meeting with Van Dyke to a member of staff in the university's Office of
Development, Peter Sylvester. Thereafter I gave the matter no further thought and discussed it with no one. In 1997, when London
media investigators were looking into Court frauds against my
company, Banner International, in Utah in 1993, they phoned Peter Sylvester as part of that investigation. I was listening in to the
call and astonished when he launched into a phenomenal diatribe
that I was obsessed with Jane Stanford having been poisoned, and
going around saying that the Stanford University President at that
time, David Starr Jordan, was responsible for her murder.

The fact was: I had mentioned my meeting with Van Dyke
to Sylvester just that once and then had completely dropped the
subject. Far from being "obsessed," I had forgotten all about it,
and knew nothing other than what I had been told in 1983. What
was going on? Was it because the Stanford and Requa families
were related? Why would Sylvester allege that I was "obsessed"
about Jane Stanford's death when I had forgotten all about it for
14 years? Very strange things were happening.

Then, out of the blue in 2001, I received that crucial email
from Dr Cutler:

Subject: jane lathrop stanford
Date: Sun, 29 Jul 2001 08:31:40 -0700 (PDT)

Dear Mr. Requa:

I obtained your e-mail address from the ubron.org website. I have just finished reading much of the interesting information posted at banner-companies.com. I will look forward to seeing your book.

I write hoping that you are the Stanford alumnus who provided information in 1983 to Peter Sylvester in the Office of Development. If you are not, you may wish to read no further. Sylvester's memorandum on the subject of your information was sent to me by the University archivist who is helping me research the death of Jane Stanford.

I am a retired Stanford neurologist.... I have just completed a book on the history of magnesite mining in my home town (Livermore, Ca). That mine was also placed in receivership because of stock swindles in 1916. But for the last 8 months I have been researching the death of Mrs. Stanford. I have focused on the medical evidence, the physicians and toxicologists who were involved, and the efforts by David Starr Jordan to obscure what was certainly, in my view, a case of murder.

The memorandum from Sylvester states that you are (were) acquainted with Robert Van Dyke who was said to have written a lengthy manuscript documenting that Jordan and Darius Mills were involved in the death of Mrs. Stanford. I wrote to Van Dyke some time ago, but I did not receive a response (nor was my letter returned).

I wondered if you had any more information about Mrs. Stanford you might be willing to share with me, or alternatively, if you are still in contact with Van Dyke, whether you might be willing to ask if he would be agreeable to being contacted.

Any help you can provide will be greatly appreciated.

Sincerely,
Robert W.P. Cutler, MD

Such had been the facts about the Van Dyke meetings in Hawaii; and, I was amazed that a record of them had been found by Dr. Cutler in Stanford Archives. I replied as follows:

Dear Dr. Cutler:

I am overjoyed at hearing from you with your researches. I too tried to track down Van Dyke quite a few months ago, maybe about a year and a half. He has a signed statement from the boy who delivered the prescription to Mrs. Stanford at the Moana Hotel that killed her. Needless to say, Van Dyke got the statement when the boy had also become a very old man many years ago.

I will try to track him down again. I failed about a year and a half ago.

Incidentally, I am a cousin of the last Stanford, Helen Winslow Stanford. She was my father's first cousin. My grandmother's sister was Mrs. Josiah Stanford...

I'll send you my chapter on Hawaiian Days that includes my meeting with Van Dyke. I'll see what I can do to track him down for you. The value of the Stanford story lies in the moral it presents: very similar to the moral of the Banner story. It would be quite phenomenal if the University admitted to it and took Jordan's name off everything.

I guess you know that Jordan got all the Honolulu police reports. He took them back to Stanford. I wonder if they got burned or if the University still has them.

Sincerely,
Stephen Requa

Eventually, Dr. Cutler was able to get approval from the university Archivist to send me, by hard mail, a copy of that memorandum.

For more than three years thereafter I exchanged emails with Dr. Cutler – sometimes almost daily – in our mutual efforts and collaborating in our investigations. One result was his book published by the Stanford Press, *The Mysterious Death of Jane Stanford*. Its publication made front page national news, with some comments by myself, as also included in some articles.

My own book, *The Great American Gold Grab*, was published in 2009, five years after Dr. Cutler's death in 2004.

During my research with Dr. Cutler, and our exchanges of +300 emails (many with attached documents), we covered the following topics:

- His providing the Van Dyke/Archives memorandum to me;

- The details about Van Dyke and related comments and disclosures;

- His efforts and final success in contacting Van Dyke; his other Stanford-obtained information on Van Dyke;

- His many comments on researching Requa and Stanford histories;

- His many provisions of documentation about Stanford, San Francisco, and California history at that time as was related;

- His many comments on the details in my own book then in manuscript form;

- His own details and research about those facts as referred to in the Van Dyke/Sylvester memorandum;

- Details on his progress in gaining his own publication;

- My warnings to him to avoid the Stanford administration from knowing about his book that could lead to possible efforts to squelch it; most particularly my warning to avoid any Sylvester contact;

- The events of the front page media sensation after publication;

- His commiserating on my own troubles with Stanford as became evident arising from their having that Memorandum before I knew it;

- His many and varied philosophical comments in general;

- His comments on the David Starr Jordan "cult" at Stanford and his contempt for Jordan;

- His conclusion that Isaac L. Requa, my great-grandfather, then President of the Stanford-originating Central Pacific Railroad was the "obvious second victim" to the poisoning of Jane Stanford (sent in March 2004); Isaac collapsed at lunch at the Pacific Union Club a couple of days after Jane's funeral;

- Our collaboration on a film treatment for the whole story;

From his death in 2004 until 2010 I paid little added attention to the mass of documentation and emails I had compiled, except that I had my own book published in 2009. This part was written right after I completed the film treatment:

Five days later [after completion of the film treatment] – on Wednesday, April 14, 2004 – I got some shattering news from Mrs. Cutler. Bob had died suddenly and peacefully on Monday, April 12. My world suddenly became very flat and hollow.

I knew, with his emphysema, that his time was going to be curtailed, and he had e-mailed me recently that he had taken a turn for the worse. Fortunately, I had taken the opportunity to write him about how much our collaboration had meant to me. Indeed, he was like a guardian spirit, almost like a father. For almost three years he had been there, having come to me from out of the blue, to give me information that would help salvage my reputation, my life, and my career.

But he did more than that. Somehow he instinctively knew what I had been through and had been there with sometimes daily e-mails to urge me on. His findings had restored my credibility, had shattered the credibility of Stanford, and had given me new faith. His wisdom, quiet brilliance, kindness, and keen insight into my dilemmas had enveloped my daily thinking for those years. Because of him I had even been quoted on the front page of the *Los Angeles Times*, and then syndicated nation-wide.

The day I heard the news from Mrs. Cutler I felt cut adrift in a world that had again become alien. I had never found a greater kindred spirit than Dr. Robert Cutler. He had been a miracle, coming unbidden out of the blue.

As I spoke the next day with a wise friend in whom I had been confiding, he said I could look at it another way: that Dr.Cutler had stayed longer than he might otherwise have done, just to help me out. That sounded right.... He had held on right up to that very day of completion with a film treatment. Among his last and most important messages to me had been: "Get your book out." He knew that history and civilization needed these disclosures, as they had needed his about Stanford.

The events that had started in Honolulu in 1983 with Van Dyke talking to me about Darius Ogden Mills and Jordan having conspired in murdering Jane Stanford had come full circle and reached an irreversible momentum.

What Karma, I thought: that after all the things Stanford people had done to ruin me, I would end up with a film treatment on the details of Jane Stanford's murder that included a possible case of murder complicity against the university itself.

At the time of the front page news coverage I received the following from my lawyer Dr. William F. Pepper:

Dear Stephen,

First of all let me commend you on the work you have done with respect to the death of Mrs Stanford. It is clear to me that you have opened a can of worms and set out a very credible case of apparent murder based upon the Cutler evidence. Your diligence serves well the Stanford family and, although they do not realize it at this time, the entire Stanford community. Of course, I can only urge you to follow through with this work. There is, as you know, no statute of limitations involving murder. I have no doubt that it is a potentially very worrying matter for the university.

As ever, W.F. Pepper

The interviews by London journalists in 1997 showed that ever since 1983 corrupted Stanford administrators had been very worried about me. A phenomenal libel campaign had been instigated against me in 1993 at Stanford and elsewhere; and the discoveries about the scope of events around and after Jane Stanford's death would mushroom beyond what I could imagine.

To my thinking, there appears to be a clear and continuous line of crimes deriving from Jane Stanford's poisoning, and that of my great-grandfather Isaac, and it all connects into one timeline from the 1905 poisonings through the organization and passage of the Federal Reserve Act, and beyond

Key figures in the poisoning death of Jane Stanford in 1905 were David Starr Jordan and Darius Ogden Mills. Looming in the background were Pres. Theodore Roosevelt, John D. Rockefeller, and Whitelaw Reid, who along with his father-in-law Darius Ogden Mills arrived in California just as Jane Stanford's death in Hawaii was announced. My research has shown that many of these same people were also involved in the horrifying eugenics movement, but there was still very much more for me to learn.

The day before the 1905 Hawaii inquest ruling of death by strychnine poisoning, Whitelaw Reid was appointed Ambassador to the Court of St. James (U.K.) by President Teddy Roosevelt. At that moment he was also serving as an executor for Jane Stanford, but I can find no record of Whitelaw Reid and Jane Stanford having ever even met. He lived 3000 miles away in New York City. He served in London until 1912 where he died. That same year Roosevelt was well paid by the bankers to stand as 'Bull Moose' candidate against President William Taft and Democrat candidate, Woodrow Wilson. The popular President Taft had refused to support the Aldrich Plan for a central bank because it offered only nominal government control and would place the bankers in the driver's seat. As intended, Roosevelt split the Republican vote in 1912 and ensured that Taft failed to make a second term. The path had carefully been cleared for Woodrow Wilson – a political captive of Wall Street bankers who had agreed to their hidden agenda – to gain the Presidency and sign off on the corrupt Federal Reserve Act.

Whitelaw Reid's tenure as U.S. Ambassador to the U.K. may have been for purposes of liaising with the Rothschild banking cartel on the terms for the Federal Reserve Act. I was discovering this history while I was seeking to counter a libel campaign against me and my mining interests. Sylvester's 1983 Memorandum had clearly started something major at Stanford. In his phone call with the investigators in 1997, while egregiously lying about me, he sounded a bit desperate.

Twenty years later with Cutler in 2003, I found a university web site that was entirely based on the details provided by Van Dyke to me that were the basis for Sylvester's Memo of 1983. Stanford had been stewing on those things that they had learned just from me in 1983 and that they were trying to debunk on-line twenty years later. Something in that Sylvester Memo of 1983 had struck a very raw nerve with the higher administration. With Cutler's data in all his emails to me, I finally figured out what it was – but not until 2016. It will hopefully mean the end of corrupt control of Stanford University and the restoration of the Stanford University as Jane Stanford had intended before those who stole it in 1904/1905 then murdered her and Isaac Requa.

All the libel campaigns against me now appeared to be derived in whole or in major part from an epicenter at Stanford. Were they worried about what I would reveal regarding David Starr Jordan and the university's role in Jane Stanford's murder, and that Isaac Requa had also been one of their victims?

Maybe they were not worried about Jane Stanford's death exposures per se, but about what I might find if that was looked into: perhaps about institutionalized eugenics (i.e. Nazi eugenics) and that it was also the very same people who organized and passed the Federal Reserve Banking Act. Some strong evidence shows the bankers bribed TR Roosevelt with $100 million "donated" to a eugenics organization to swing the 1912 election, insure a Wilson victory, and his signature on the Federal Reserve Act. Later, Wilson rued his actions, and had this to say:

> A great industrial nation is controlled by its system of credit. Our system of credit is privately concentrated. The growth of the nation, therefore, and all our activities are in the hands of a few men ... [W]e have come to be one of the worst ruled, one of the most completely controlled and dominated, governments in the civilized world – no longer a government by free opinion, no longer a government by conviction and the vote of the majority, but a government by the opinion and the duress of small groups of dominant men.

But there is more to it than that. Some of this has to do with my grandfather and Herbert Hoover having been brought together as the world's leading mining engineers, with the seeming ultimate plan of monopolization of gold mining and control of gold reserves by the very same crowd, perhaps after they had reduced the value of the dollar to almost nil? Gold in 1912 was $20 per ounce. Now it is over $1200. Looks like the "banksters" knew what they were doing in bringing Mark L. Requa and Herbert Hoover together.

The very same forces who had been involved in the poisoning of Jane Stanford and Isaac Requa later organized for Isaac's son Mark, my grandfather, and Herbert Hoover to collect the Requa/ Hoover Files. From the early 1930s "they" organized the funding of over a hundred of million dollars for Herbert Hoover, Mark Requa, and my father, Lawrence Requa to amass the exclusive Requa/Hoover Files, which covered thousands of mining properties throughout the Western Hemisphere.

The task was complete enough by the time Nixon freed the price of gold for "them" to try to obtain those files in 1974. That effort through John Paul Getty failed when I refused his overtures after his Getty Oil had acquired the data on one property, the Mercur Gold Mine in Utah, with which data Getty with Barrick Gold were able to mine a billion dollars worth of gold and take Barrick public in 1983.

But Getty's efforts to acquire all the Requa/Hoover Files failed, even after it appears that murder was resorted to in 1974 to try to break my hold on the files by trying to frame me for the murder of one Samuel Edelman in San Francisco. That failed when by happenstance I unexpectedly removed myself from the murder scene just before it transpired. Stealing the Requa/Hoover Files would then require waiting for a fraudulent receivership in Utah in 1993 about which Cutler mentioned seeing information online.

Cutler would not see the ultimate success of his research in finding the culprits of Jane Stanford's murder – aside from convincing ourselves of Jordan's and Bertha Berner's culpabilities and seeing that Issac Requa was the "obvious second victim" – but he saw the compelling criminal story of the somehow Stanford-related crimes against me and my company, Banner International, which was destroyed with the theft of the Requa/Hoover Files in the Utah court frauds of the receivership in 1993.

On March 21, 2004 Cutler wrote me as follows:

> Subject: Re: Random Thoughts on Treatment
> To: herrick_req
>
> Steven:
> I learned yesterday that Requa [Isaac] was elected Pres. of the CP at the same meeting where Huntington was elected VP. Huntington and Mrs. Stanford had some major difference. Huntington and Mills could have a connection. I'll try to flesh this out and provide a coherent synopsis of the Fur Seal stuff – my intuition is that there is not much there and it may be distracting.
>
> I think you can get Van Dyke safely in without enumerating each of his points. The affidavit, letter, missing journal pages should be enough. I had the impression that Van Dyke is severely hypochrondriacal....
>
> The chances of a forensic success with exhumation [on Isaac] depends on the poison. Most compelling are the acts

against you and Banner – focus there, bring in Stanford because it is an important element. Bring in everything you can
prove. My thoughts on some of the issues I posed are formu-
lating as follows:

    1) Since so many women and an SU professor of psychol-
ogy thinks there was a relationship between Jordan and Berner and since that would answer, most simply, many of the
questions, I tend to think the dramatization should allude or
include that…

Cutler could little have imagined the ultimate organized evils
that would surface in direct connection to the Stanford murder
timeline from 1905 through 1913 with election-rigging. Nor
would Cutler be able to see the hideous and then immediate connections of Jordan and his cohorts with eugenics – and ultimately with Nazism – to the agenda that immediately compelled the
murders.

Stanford the birthplace of Nazism? Not a farfetched notion at all!

Cutler, however, did give us his understated details of the extreme odiousness of Jordan's character, the details of which could
be made of great value in a Hollywood adaptation with Jordan as
an ultimate fiend, as a spokesperson for eugenics, and organizing
and covering up murder. The dialogue that Cutler has provided
for Jordan is priceless for its exemplary and ultimate expressions
of "human" evil.

But Jordan is in the end rather pathetic with his disgusting academic frauds of eugenics, although those were magnified to the
horrifying extreme with Nazi eugenics – not that Jordan and his
apostles of that diabolic creed didn't try to do equal things first in
the U.S. In that they proved to be amateurs to Hitler, but Jordan
gave Hitler the eugenics "blueprints" for doing what he did.

Immediately involved with Jordan, as Van Dyke unearthed in
Hawaii and told me in 1983, was Darius Ogden Mills, who didn't
go to Hawaii, although his money in bribes did. With Darius Ogden Mills we have found the veritable Darth Vader responsible
for dreaming up the whole timeline of depravity, murders, and all
else, and then for financing it, at least on the ground in California and Hawaii. But much of the higher Stanford administration
immediately knew who he was back in 1983 as soon as they read
Sylvester's Memo. That's one reason why Sylvester and much of
the upper Stanford administration was panicking and desperate,

all the way from 1983 up to the Utah Court Frauds in 1993 to destroy Banner International and steal its Requa/Hoover Files. It is clear that some at Stanford had jumped into bed with various syndicates of organized crime; clear why Sylvester was panicking in 1997 and telling people I was obsessed with Jane Stanford's death and should be ignored.

But unbeknownst to me at that time, what Sylvester and senior Stanford administrators were really panicking about – and trying to destroy me for – what I might reveal about Darius Ogden Mills. He was the "Founder" of the present Stanford University in 1905 after he organized and paid for the murders of Jane Stanford and Isaac Requa, while lining Jordan up with the Rockefellers and Rothschilds and Teddy Roosevelt. He had been doing high-level banking business for more than 20 years with the Rothschilds; and, most of all with Harriman and the Rothschilds he wanted Isaac Requa's Central Pacific Railroad to merge with their Southern Pacific Railroad.

Darius Ogden Mills is indeed the Darth Vader of our story, with whose exposures we may now bring down the Evil Empire – while we restore the authentic Stanford University as founded by Leland and Jane Stanford back in 1885 to its rightful status before they murdered Jane to steal it – or rather they murdered Jane Stanford to keep what they had already just stolen, as Professor Julius Goebel has clarified to us from 1904.

Now we must thank Dr. Robert W.P. Cutler, M.D. This volume is dedicated to that wonderful human being; to bringing his spirit and his work to life again and enable him to say publically the things he said privately to me in his many emails. I publish them in the fervent hope that they will awaken the Stanford community – and far beyond – to the evil charades promulgated by the bankers. We can rid ourselves of their power, their suffocating control and their warmongering by dismantling the remnants of David Starr Jordan on the Stanford campus and all those who were/are similarly corrupting other great American institutions. Bob Cutler, I know for sure, would approve.

Stephen Herrick Requa
London
July 14, 2016

RECEIVED

JUL 1 1 1983

Vice President for
Public Affairs

DATE: July 11, 1983

To : Robert E. Freelen
Vice President for Public Affairs

FROM : Peter Sylvester
Office of Development

SUBJECT: "Murder at the Moana" by Robert Van Dyke

Dear Bob:

Confirming our telephone conversation, Van Dyke, a Honolulu "free-lance historian" is said to have written an extensive manuscript identifying David Starr Jordan and Darius Ogden Mills as conspirators in the 2/28/05 poisoning of Jane Stanford. My informant, alumnus Steve Requa, has had several visits with Van Dyke because of their mutual interest in Hawaiian history. Reportedly wealthy, Van Dyke owns a private archive of rare books and paintings on Pacific and Hawaiian history, including the Ray Jerome Baker collection of Hawaiian History, as well as film footage of the last Queen's funeral, etc. He is reported to be in his mid-forties, a bit eccentric, and still under the influence of his mother.

Van Dyke told Requa that a major TV network had offered to buy television rights to his Jane Stanford manuscript to be used as the basis for a miniseries, "Murder at the Moana" (the hotel in which Mrs. Stanford died). He further said that he had fifty "new" pieces of historical evidence bearing on Mrs. Stanford's death. He mentioned two items specifically: 1) a signed statement by the boy (now an old man) who was sent to the drugstore to get medicine for Jane Stanford, was intercepted by someone, and persuaded to get cyanide instead; 2) a letter from Jordan to some Hawaiian relatives of Jane Stanford (Cartwrights?) thanking them for their help in dispatching Mrs. Stanford. He also mentioned that Dr. Jordan had picked up the Honolulu police report on Mrs. Stanford's death and "lost" it en route to California.

Perhaps, as you suggested, the Stanford Historical Society will have an interest in contacting Van Dyke. While it's hard to believe that Van Dyke has come up with anything new, it's true that the circumstances of Mrs. Stanford's death surface periodically as an unsolved mystery.

By the way, I asked Requa if he thought Van Dyke had been in contact with anyone at Stanford and he replied that perhaps a local, Hawaiian alumnus had been to see him. Requa added that Van Dyke's interest seemed to be to "vindicate" Mrs. Stanford (whatever that means), and not to cause trouble or turn a profit. Van Dyke has not decided what to do with the manuscript according to Requa, and would consult his mother before reaching a decision to make it public.

P.E.S.

cc; Bill Dailey
Dave Fulton
PES working files

OD File: Stephen H. Requa (This was cut off)

Robert Cutler, M.D., had first made contact with me after he found in the Stanford University archives a copy of a memorandum in 1983 written by Peter Sylvester to various high administration officials. In his memo Sylvester brought up the issues that I had reported to him after returning to campus from Hawaii, where I had discussed the matter with historian Robert Van Dyke. Cutler tracked me down on the Web and we began an intensive, almost daily, e-mail exchange for about two years.

Chapter I

The Cliff-Hanger with Stanford University Press

My intensive three year exchanges with Dr. Cutler began on July 29, 2001, starting first, with issues about Peter Sylvester who had written the Memorandum of 1983 that Cutler had found in Stanford University Archives. Robert Van Dyke, the subject of that memorandum, was our second concern. He had made the allegations about his evidence for David Starr Jordan and Darius Ogden Mills being behind the poisoning of Jane Stanford in Honolulu. Our third set of initial concerns was with the mechanics of the poisoning in Hawaii. On September 13, 2002, I got word (below) from Cutler that he had signed the contract with Stanford University Press to publish the book that had thus evolved. I could hardly believe it! I had given the chance of it being published at Stanford as almost nil. But I got the surprise of a lifetime with this:

> To: Stephen Herrick Requa
> Subject: Jane Stanford
> Date: Fri, 13 Sep 2002 13:50:14 -0700 (PDT)
>
> Dear Stephen,
> Well, I've just signed a contract with Stanford to publish my book, so that is done.
> I want to thank you for all of your support throughout this project. I will be very interested to learn how your affairs are progressing when you have the time.
>
> Best wishes, Robert

It had indeed been a cliff-hanger for us both leading up to this, with my own rather certain expectations that somehow the university administration would ascertain what was going on with him at the Press and somehow scuttle it, or just stomp on it with all their might.

The first thing I had done was to tell Cutler, by no means, to contact Peter Sylvester, who I found had been grossly libeling me and alleged that I had been obsessed with the issue. The emails from Cutler leading up to the signing indicate the cliff-hanger feelings for both of us.

Word of a possible definite "Go" had come earlier on August 14:

> To Stephen Herrick Requa
> 14/08/2002
>
> Dear Stephen:
>
> It looks like you have been busy indeed! Congratulations on orchestrating these important projects to near completion.
>
> Last evening, Norris Pope, Editor in Chief of SU Press called me to apologize for the long delays and to inform me that my book has been approved for publication (contract still on the way – people on vacation). But it is definitely a GO. The marketing folks think the market may be restricted to the Stanford community (quite large in my view), and they are going to publish it as a cloth covered hardback in the scholarly work category. Pope thinks the market is bigger and is happy to re-issue as a trade paperback if he is proven correct. My delivery date is Sept. 15 which I can easily meet. I still know nothing about film rights, etc., but of course I haven't signed anything.
>
> As of now, I am pleased with the outcome. I need a better title, but I think you can refer to the book as "forthcoming." Thanks for your support. Will keep you posted.
>
> Best, Robert

A prior email concerning the Stanford Press had been this:

> Sent: 27 July 2002 14:30:49
> To: Stephen Herrick Requa (sherrickrequa@hotmail.com)
>
> Glad to hear your documentary is moving along.
>
> I would be most pleased to talk to someone on your crew about Mrs. Stanford. We now have a regular telephone line and my number is (925) XXX-XXXX.

The "couple of weeks" SU Press estimated to draw up a contract is approaching two months so I will probably give them a call next week. People in academics don't usually work very hard in the summer; hopefully the delay is no more than that.

I hope you are finding time to finish your book and also that Banner is going well.

Best, Robert

I was keeping Cutler aware of the prospect for obstruction from the Office of Development:

From: Stephen Herrick Requa
Sent: 06 June 2002 10:00:15
To: rwpcutler33@yahoo.com

Hi Robert:

I read your new chapter and found it very interesting. I've been meaning to reply but have been very busy lately. I'd like to read the chapter again and see if I can have anything more or less well informed to say. Has the Press made any further communication? Otherwise, any sign of the Men in Black from the Office of Development?

Regards, Stephen

Before this I had received a missive that mentioned the very important work of Professor Carnochan who had dug up decisive evidence about Professor Julius Goebel, a friend of Jane Stanford.

From: robert cutler
To: Stephen Herrick Requa
Subject: Re: Hello
Date: Tue, 21 May 2002 09:00:21 -0700 (PDT)

Dear Stephen:

I have been meaning to write to thank you for the materials on Banner. I hope that enterprise is developing in the manner you expect and deserve. I particularly hope you are finding time to work on your book – getting our two books out in the same time frame could be mutually beneficial. I have not heard from the Press, and I have given myself till the end of the month before I contact my friend C---------to see what he can learn. The book could well be making some Stanford folk nervous, or perhaps, like all publishing companies they are just slow. As you probably know, most university presses find themselves in a position of needing to make a living; subsidies from their parents are dwindling. Heretofore, Stanford Press has published "field-related" scholarly books only. Now they need to have a line the purpose of which is to make them money, and I think my book falls into that category. For that reason, I believe runs and promotion will be executed for their advantage (and ultimately mine). We'll see. In the meantime, I am working on an extra chapter which I know will be wanted by the Press – on the case of Professor Ross. It was the mismanagement of Jordan's firing of Professor Ross that started the serious rift between Mrs. Stanford and Jordan.

Be assured I will let you know of developments at SU.

Best regards,
Robert

The first indication and news that Stanford Press had wanted to publish the book had come three weeks before:

From: Stephen Herrick Requa 01 April 2002 01:11:22
To: rwpcutler33@

Robert:

I am amazed about the Editor wanting to publish the book, considering the powerful spin doctors and fund raisers at Stanford, who would like to see this issue buried forever. It's a testament to your medical acumen, clear thinking, judicious approach, restraint, and comprehensive research. Sylvester, who was ridiculing the idea in 1993 and using the issue to discredit me (for ulterior motives of the Office of Development and some of their donors who were involved in the schemes against Banner) will be pretty red-faced soon, as in bright red.

Congratulations indeed! It's so good to see integrity and diligence rewarded. It's also a good statement for the integrity of the Stanford Press. Now if I can hone my book into a final edit as judicious as yours.

Many thanks to Aaron for his library work on Isaac Requa. Again, well deserved congratulations.

Regards
Stephen

Until this news, Cutler had been waiting for a review from the forensic pathologist. He notes that if his book is scuttled, I had warned him:

From: robert cutler <rwpcutler33@>
To: Stephen Herrick Requa
Subject: Re: Reply
Date: Thu, 28 Mar 2002 13:28:16 -0800 (PST)

Stephen -

Good to hear from you. I hope your financial ventures are proceeding satisfactorily. Has your writing been put on hold by these necessary activities? My son, Aaron, was happy to do the library work and wants no remuneration. Arsenic is cumulative and can poison over a long period, but it produces a severe peripheral neuropathy and a characteristic skin rash resembling a pattern of rain droplets on dusty skin.

The forensic pathologist gave my manuscript a thumbs up and a strong recommendation to publish. I just learned this about two weeks ago. We now await a review by "a Stanford historian" which should be forthcoming soon. The Editor of the Press says he wants to publish my book. Hopefully, it won't get scuttled, but if it is, you warned me. I would like to get this done with soon. Hope everything is well.

All the best,
Robert

Prior to these exchanges Cutler and I had been focusing on the more serious factual issues of the poisoning details per se in Hawaii and on the various issues of Robert Van Dyke. Cutler wondered how Van Dyke had been onto the case to start with. By July 2002, Cutler had ascertained the probability behind that as he wrote:

From: robert cutler (rwpcutler33@)
Sent: 07 July 2002 07:58:37
To: Stephen Herrick Requa

Dear Stephen:

I have long wondered why Van Dyke would have regaled
you with stories of Mrs. Stanford's death in 1983, nearly 80
years after the event took place. As far as I knew, it was not
the talk of the town for all of those years. I have recently
learned, however, that an article published in the obscure
journal, *Pacific Historian*, by Gary Ogle in 1981 (the first to
conclude poisoning and to expose Jordan's cover-up) was
reprinted in the *Pacific Commercial Advertiser* in Honolulu
on July 27, 1981, complete with pictures and old headlines.
Possibly that is what piqued Van Dyke's interest.

Best,
Robert

Back on August 3, 2001 I had received Cutler's word that he
had received permission from Stanford Archives to send Sylvester's memorandum to me. Again I warned him against passing on
to Sylvester that we were in communication. I felt that information would surely nix the book's publication:

03/08/2001
To rwpcutler33@

Robert:
Just a cautionary note again to advise that you tell as few
people as possible about your manuscript or any publishing intentions. Obviously Sylvester was trying to curry favor
with the University over this, and other people would be
inclined to do the same. Another reason for getting it published outside the US and far away from Stanford. Regards,

Stephen

At the same time Cutler had got word from the archivist that
he could forward me a copy of the Sylvester memorandum:

From: robert cutler <rwpcutler33@>
To: Stephen Herrick Requa

Subject: memo
Date: Fri, 3 Aug 2001 08:04:33 -0700 (PDT)

Dear Steven,

I have received the necessary permission and now attach (hopefully) the memo on the Van Dyke matter. My equipment is antiquated and I see the copier has dropped characters and distorted fonts. But I think it's readable. My Honolulu contact is away so I have nothing to report on the Van Dyke collection, or the man himself. I certainly don't mistrust your use of my manuscript and will send it to you fairly soon. I am awaiting a couple of pieces of information that will allow me to finish it. I warn you there is a bit of medicine in it, but I don't think it is overwhelming. Give me another month, or longer if we find the Van Dyke files.

Best regards,
Robert

A day later I added this in another email:

Your hurdle is to get it out in print, independently, without people making problems for you – which they WILL do, just to curry favor with whomever they can rile up in the University against you. That is what it appears Sylvester perhaps did to me – in alliance with those whom I was about to expose in some serious violations of securities laws.

But as time has proved, behind it was much more than securities laws violations. It was about issues at the very jugular of Stanford University ever since it was taken over by a coup in 1905, under whom in very important respects it has remained subservient as exemplified by Condoleezza Rice, a Stanford mentor and proponent of Bush's war-profiteering agendas. Another flagrant in-your-face action along this line was Stanford's appointment of Donald Rumsfeld as a "Distinguished Visiting Scholar" in 2007.

More to indicate the pervasive reality of Stanford having been taken over by the moneyed "elite" in 1905 after the poisoning of Jane Stanford and Isaac Requa – and Stanford remaining taken over to this day – was reflected in 1980 when Stanford President Richard Lyman retired, and then ran right off to head the Rockefeller Foundation.

"[A] great evil at the heart of the myth," as I was quoted on the front page of the *Los Angeles Times*, has remained intact since Jane Stanford was poisoned in 1905. Along with a "cover up," which called the poisoning "heart disease," which almost everyone knew was a transparent lie, but everyone sat still for. They knew they weren't really fooling anyone; they intimidated them into silence.

In 2001 with Cutler, our exchanges on the issues themselves about Van Dyke and the poisoning per se in Honolulu began. His first words about tracking down Van Dyke were these:

> From: robert cutler (rwpcutler33@)
> Sent: 05 October 2001 09:06:21
> To: Stephen Herrick Requa
>
> Stephen,
>
> Glad to hear from you. I hope your major strides include the many endeavors in which you are engaged, including, of course, your book. I am still working on mine, mostly digesting newspaper accounts at present. Here's the status on Van Dyke (from whom I have never heard): He sold his collection of photographs and historical documents to the Bishop Estate in 1996 for $422,831. A Bishop librarian, Sigrid Southworth spent about 7 months sorting through the stuff, and an attorney, Albert Jeremiah spent further months finishing an inventory. Southworth does not remember encountering anything about Mrs. Stanford. I have written to Jeremiah but have not had a response. So, we'll see, and I'll certainly keep you posted.
>
> Best wishes, Robert

His next news about Van Dyke was this:

> From: robert cutler (rwpcutler33@)
> Sent: 31 October 2001 08:22:41
> To: Stephen Herrick Requa

Hello Stephen,

It's going ok, thank you. I don't have the facility for writing that you seem to possess so I do it one word at a time. How is your book coming – near the publication stage? What is its title? How is it going to be received at The University?

I think since I last wrote that I have learned that the Stanford Historical Society (i.e. Nilan on the memo I sent you) did not pursue looking for Van Dyke. He apparently visited the Stanford library at least once, because the archivist knew of him.

I hope when I receive a bit more outstanding information to be able to close this project. I fear you will find it a bit dull compared to your own project. If nothing else, I hope it sets the record straight that Mrs. Stanford was murdered and that Jordan was not the hero Stanford made of him, at least in this case.

Keep me posted and best wishes, Robert

About the dovetailing of our work and information, Cutler wrote:

From: robert cutler <rwpcutler33@>
To: Stephen Herrick Requa
Subject: a request
Date: Fri, 7 Dec 2001 15:55:55 -0800 (PST)

Dear Stephen,

I've been meaning to write to inquire how your mining projects are progressing. I hope the prospects are now under study and that the litigation in which you are involved is also proceeding satisfactorily.

I have essentially completed my small book. It is a factual account and shows the efforts taken by Jordan to cover things up. It includes some speculation as to why. I find I cannot bring myself to say he was covering his own ass, but readers can draw inferences. In doing some final editing today, it occurred to me the inferences could be more obvious if I could make some sort of reference to your book. I wondered how the attached endnote strikes you. If you do not approve, please do not hesitate to tell me. I do not want to steal your thunder, but on the other hand, if Stanford would publish my book, it would call attention to yours. If you do approve, I will need the title of your book and verification that "in press" is ok. My manuscript is now about 135 pages. I intend to send you a hard copy, probably next week, and when you have the time, I would be very interested in your comments.

Best regards, Robert

A week later I received an email that included leads that ten years later would be vital in my understanding, especially about Darius Ogden Mills and Whitelaw Reid. Giving credence to Van Dyke's claims, Cutler noted that Darius Ogden Mill was "in town" and at Stanford at that time, but he didn't "know why."

Cutler speculated on a connection between Mills and the Requas at that time, and in fact Mills had financed the Eureka Palisade Railroad with Isaac Requa. Mills had been the richest man in California until he moved to New York City, where he became father-in-law of Whitelaw Reid. I posited, later, that Reid and Mills had hopped a train in New York making a bee-line to Stanford – arriving just in time for Jane Stanford's demise to be announced. Cutler mentions Reid serving "later [as] Ambassador to England." I was to ascertain, that "later" was just a *few days later*. Reid was appointed ambassador on March 8, 1905, the day before the Inquest and Coroner's Verdict of death by strychnine had been announced in Hawaii.

I feel that was the last day his appointment could have been made in light of the circumstances, Reid being the "executor" to a woman who the next day would be adjudicated having been murdered. No evidence has been found as to how or why Reid might genuinely have been Jane Stanford's executor. He lived 3,000 miles away, and there is no record of them ever having met.

Unlike Whitelaw Reid, Timothy Hopkins, a Stanford University trustee, accompanied Jordan to Hawaii to recover Mrs. Stanford's body. While he was there the Honolulu newspapers, as covered in Cutler's book, reported that Hopkins tried to bribe the autopsy doctors and toxicologists into dropping their verdict of strychnine poisoning.

From: robert cutler (rwpcutler33@)
Sent: 14 December 2001 11:51:51
To: Stephen Herrick Requa

Stephen:

I have a copy of the Stanford will. Two million in trust to one of her brothers, one million to another, various sums to charities, $15k to Berner and $1k to various servants. Residue, including jewels, paintings, object d'arts, etc. to Stanford trustees. What I don't know is what the residue amounted to, but I doubt if it was more than $1-2 million. Most of the Stanford endowment had been established in 1903. I don't believe there would have been any financial incentive here for Jordan. Some relatives on Leland's side were interviewed by reporters (I don't have exactly who at my fingertips) and were said to have no resentment that they were not remembered in the will.

Darius Ogden Mills was an early banking, railroad, mining tycoon friend of Leland (and possibly the Requas) – started the Bank of California and the town of Milbrae. He lived in NY, and I don't know why he was in town around the time of Mrs. Stanford's death save that he had a mansion in Milbrae. He died a few years later. Whitelaw Reid was Mill's son-in-law. He was the editor of the *NY Tribune*, later Ambassador to England, and a trustee of SU. Timothy Hopkins was adopted son of Mark Hopkins. His adopted mother, on the death of her husband, married a man about 20-25 years her junior. When she died, new husband got her money. Hopkins contested the will and won a good sum.

Do you recall exactly the circumstances of your meeting Van Dyke and why he chose to tell you this stuff? As I think I must have mentioned (my memory could be better), he did sell a collection of material to the Bishop School through a private deal with one of the trustees. It has been in the courts for years, because the rest of the trustees had turned him down. I have correspondence that a librarian at the Bishop Schools worked on the collection for nine months. She saw nothing pertaining to Mrs. Stanford. An attorney was hired to complete the inventory. I corresponded with him and received no response. There is a lot of controversy about the Van Dyke collection and about Van Dyke himself.

I don't know how long it would take to get pictures from old newspapers. I don't even know just how I would go about it, although it must be possible. About 25 pictures would cover the people and places.

Robert

A few days later Cutler wrote about one of the most important issues: where the strychnine in the bicarbonate of soda had come from. Did it arrive with the bicarbonate from California? Was it put into the bicarbonate in Hawaii, or was the bicarbonate purchased in Hawaii and delivered with the strychnine added? Van Dyke had stated that a boy in Hawaii had delivered it from a pharmacy. If so, the strychnine came from Hawaii.

It was crucial, however, for Jordan and Berner to maintain that the bicarbonate came from San Francisco and that the strychnine had thus had its origin there. This was of significant importance in getting the police investigation focused not on Hawaii (less corruptible to them), but on San Francisco where Darius Ogden Mills was on hand with plentiful money to corrupt and stifle any competent investigation. Van Dyke through his own investigation in Hawaii alleging Darius Ogden Mills as a conspirator gives credibility to the rest of Cutler's assertions. How would he have determined this, or even thought of it, from Hawaii? Mills must have left some "footprints" with the people in Hawaii. Was Mills the paymaster? Was his purpose in going to California and Stanford to be the money man to bribe away any loose ends? To arrange the bribes required to accomplish the poisoning of Isaac Requa two days after Jane Stanford's funeral? These issues are reflected in Cutler's email:

From: robert cutler <rwpcutler33@>
To: Stephen Herrick Requa
Subject: Re: Van Dyke and Berner
Date: Mon, 17 Dec 2001 13:51:32 -0800 (PST)

Stephen:

Neither Berner nor Hunt testified about where the bicarbonate was purchased. They said it came with them packed in Stanford's favorite refillable bottle. A Palo Alto pharmacist disclosed in early March that he had sold it to them a week or so before they left. He was told they had a bottle to put it in and sold them a packet. The bottle of bicarbonate sat in an open room for nearly a week before they left. The room was accessible to all the servants (and probably others). The toxicologists measured the strychnine content in five capsules of cascara that they combined. Of course, if Berner put the capsule on the dresser, she could have pulled one from her pocket. But in my opinion, the bicarb had enough to kill an elderly person. The bottle containing the cascara capsules had an original prescription date of 1901 if I recall. The Honolulu newspapers reported that early in their investigation the police checked for strychnine sales in Honolulu. Remember, the Poland water contained nux vomica, the bicarb. pure strychnine. Berner certainly changed her story over time, but I think she did that in travel tales as well. I am told her accounts of Mrs. Stanford are not thought to be very accurate. I won't disclose either the memo or you to anyone. Some time ago, I inquired of former SU Archivist Nilan (top of memo) to see if she had followed up on the Sylvester memo copied to her. She said she had not, but she also added that Van Dyke had visited the Stanford archives (she did not remember just when)... Why would he have visited Stanford do you suppose? I still think he's our key. Maybe he would respond to a letter from you. I have his address as: ------------. He never answered but neither was my letter returned.

Robert

To this I replied as follows:

From: Stephen Herrick Requa
Sent: 18 December 2001 02:43:33
To: rwpcutler33@y

Robert:

I agree that Van Dyke and his evidence are top priority. I will try writing him. I didn't know we had an address for him. We should try to send someone around to see him. When did Van Dyke visit the archives?????
    That could be an important clue! ... I did very much get the feeling that he was sincere and his evidence probably authentic. What he said rang true. About the bicarb bought in Palo Alto, I suppose there could have been any number of reasons why Mrs. Stanford might have wanted a new supply. It might have got lost or spilled. And, of course, maybe she got worried about it after the Poland water. If I had just been poisoned I would start suspecting anything and everything that I was consuming. Was it only Berner that testified to the bicarb being on a table for a long time?

I don't think any competent killer would have bought the strychnine on record. I also believe that there had to have been a few people, more than just Jordan, in on the plot.

If Van Dyke's evidence is authentic then Mrs. Stanford, or Berner, probably ordered some bicarb, and someone knew what was transpiring and was ready to intercept the delivery [as per the boy's testimony to Van Dyke]. Very frustrating to know that there was a murder and the solution to it is so evasive.

Regards,
Stephen Requa

I then made a breakthrough in getting a telephone number for Van Dyke in Honolulu. I informed Cutler of this with the following comments:

From: Stephen Herrick Requa
Sent: 11 January 2002 04:17:34
To: rwpcutler33@

Robert:

I guess what I will do, sometime soon, about Van Dyke is give him a call to try to ascertain the following:

1) If he really does have the statement from the boy and can locate it as well as the manuscript;

2) What the alleged Darius Ogden Mills connection was;

3) If he has just been out of touch with these issues (while increasingly in ill health) and has let his papers get disorganized over the past 18 years;

4) If the alleged letter from Jordan to Emerson can be located from the family he gave it back to or can be substantiated by them. I think he said Emerson's family destroyed it;

5) If his efforts in this whole affair are/were inflated with wishful thinking or fabrication;

6) If there was something purely opportunistic about it;

7) If he is or was delusional;

8) If by a remote chance, on the other hand, he is now backtracking under some agreement or inducement, or from adverse pressure.

In 1983 he certainly seemed thoughtful and sensible and since he never got in touch with me again I presume he had no particular ulterior motive then regarding myself. Maybe after the funding here is completed we can send someone over to Honolulu to see if they can prompt and/or assist him with his "warehouses" of documentation.

Regards,
Stephen

I then did manage to connect with Van Dyke and replied to Cutler in an email entitled: "Bingo"

From: Stephen Herrick Requa
Sent: 09 January 2002 02:59:03
To: rwpcutler33@

Robert:
Well, I just spoke with Van Dyke for about half an hour. His number is 808-XXX-XXXX It's listed under ——— ——— —. He's obviously a wealth of information. The boy who was allegedly involved in the poisoning was the son of one of the ladies who worked at the Moana. The letter of Jordan was to Nathaniel B. Emerson, a police surgeon whose diary had six pages torn out corresponding to the Stanford investigation. Jordan's letter to him thanked him for his cooperation and keeping certain things confidential. Unfortunately, Van Dyke returned that letter to the family and he doesn't have a copy.

You can assess what he has to say far better than can I. He recalls getting two letters (presumably from you) but was unsure whether the requests for information were for friendly purposes. I doubt very much, based on our conversation, that he has been influenced to sit on things. I think if anything, he's concerned about his own safety. He got a lot of negative reactions to his investigations. He thinks Berner was probably influenced as well as some other male companion (?) of Mrs. Stanford's party.

His manuscript still exists and he has apparently dug up a few things more. I told him you would probably be happy to send him your manuscript and that he should trust you implicitly. I told him I'd pass his number on to you and that you'd probably call soon.

He's quite willing to talk in some detail and your first
route should be to get as much out of him on the phone as
possible, then try to get his manuscript after you've established some rapport and after he's had a chance to read your
work. He's had three heart attacks recently.

Cheers,
Stephen

Van Dyke, in pointing to Darius Ogden Mills being a key conspirator, gives much credibility to his other assertions. Van Dyke
did not know, as Cutler had found out, that Mills was "in town"
when Jane was reported dead, and thus Van Dyke must have had
other reasons for Mills to be involved, reasons he could only have
found out in context of his other discoveries in Hawaii. We must
thus also concur with Van Dyke in context of the broad conspiracy now evident in both Hawaii and in California that the strychnine did originate in Hawaii and that it was simply placed into
the different batch of bicarbonate that the boy reportedly had
delivered to Berner. The Hawaii strychnine was pure strychnine,
not nux vomica as had contaminated the Poland Water, so it was
not from the same batch of poison. It could also only have been
delivered to Berner at the Moana Hotel with careful arrangement
so that she alone, without being seen, would take delivery of it.
Van Dyke's comments in Hawaii and later by phone seem to make
one thing clear. He was receiving a lot "of negative response" to
his investigation. This could only have come from someone who
knew about the conspiracy and knew the scale of the conspiracy
– that Darius Ogden Mills was involved.

Was Van Dyke's revelations about Mills behind his receiving
intense negative reactions? It also appears very noteworthy that
the six pages of journal that disappeared were from the police surgeon's diary, along with the letter the surgeon had received from
Jordan giving him some sort of thanks. Van Dyke may have found
some fantastic evidence from among his old money friends, which
then led to all the other evidence he tracked down. Not only was
Van Dyke's investigation the object of some negative pressure, but
the statement in 1983 that his mother's approval was necessary
is also indicative. These things had been found out through their
joint "old money" circle of long-time friends. In fact, Van Dyke's
interest in 1983 was to leave the Islands.

He appears to have wanted to make a splash and then disappear to parts unknown. First, he wanted to sell his manuscript, "Murder at the Moana" as the basis for a TV series. He may have sought to do so and got another "negative" reaction. So Van Dyke was certainly stalled after 1983. Interestingly, Stanford University did not contact Van Dyke after my disclosures to Sylvester – he wrote a memo.

Did the Stanford administration know that Jane Stanford was poisoned and continue the over-a-century-long cover-up? Even in his memorandum Sylvester referred to "the poisoning" of Jane Stanford, not to a "reported" or "alleged" one, but to "the" poisoning. He also wrote that it is hard to imagine that Van Dyke had come up with "something new." Did Sylvester, along with all other recipients of his memo, ascertain that he had come up with something, perhaps not "new," but something old and real? Obviously then, they were not going to send some Stanford hack around to see Van Dyke. What they appear to have done was to ascertain the exact source(s) Van Dyke had developed and would have put pressure on them – to put that pressure on Van Dyke to desist.

Van Dyke did not sell his manuscript for a TV series and stayed in Honolulu; and, later, when he did try to sell his historical collection for almost half-a-million dollars he encountered problems. Possibly, "they" did not want him to have funds. Van Dyke having had a "lot of controversy generated around him," as Cutler reported to be the case, is just what one can expect.

He apparently went to Stanford, possibly to get more supportive evidence. But then, in the intervening years, he had three heart attacks. When I called out of the blue eighteen years after meeting him he was, however, still fresh and related the same account he had given me in 1983, plus some additional details. But then, as he contemplated a call from Cutler he would perhaps have done so with trepidation, given all the "controversy" and negative reactions that had accumulated since 1983. After my email about my conversation with Van Dyke, Cutler then also called him. His full email concerning that call should not be detailed for now, but the following was included:

From: robert cutler <rwpcutler33@>
To: Stephen Herrick Requa
Subject: Re: Note on Van Dyke

Date: Fri, 11 Jan 2002 07:52:53 -0800 (PST)

Stephen:

Good news about your financial support re mining. I hope it concludes well. My guess about Van Dyke is that your social portrayal is correct.... He told me that he had no idea where the affidavit was. I think he said he might try to find his manuscript but not with great promise. [He seems to have retracted his certainty of being able to do so after my call]. Yet he was so quick to tell me that he had shown it to a rare book dealer, that I think he has some jottings that may or may not have been polished into a manuscript. Whether this man actually frightened him, I'm not sure. To be able to answer our questions with such facility implies to me that he had given the case more than casual thought. On the Emerson family: he told me the doctor had one son, the one who showed him the journal, who is dead. He said there were no direct descendants.

I completely forgot about Darius Mills (who would also figure into Isaac Requa's story perhaps) and failed to ask him. If you are going to ask him all of those things, ask him about his sale to the Bishop Estate and whether he thinks the missing items might be in that collection. That would give us something to pressure attorney Jeremiah with. I'll let you know when I hear from SU Libraries.

Best, Robert

This fitted my own assessment of Van Dyke. He had at one time had this manuscript, and probably still did as he had told me days before, and maybe the affidavit too, and possibly had the items relative to Emerson, and all the other items he had been attentively collecting since. I missed an opportunity to quiz Van Dyke further. But this was just at the time Cutler was getting approvals from the Stanford Press. It was too late for its pending publication to attempt to resurrect Van Dyke's collection, and it did appear that he had had some considerable negative pressures put on him in a number of ways. The "steam" seemed to have gone out of his fervor since 1983, when he told me his objective was to "vindicate" Jane Stanford. This, however, continues to be a renewed objective, now given new and much greater life with Robert Cutler's book. Thanks to him we know with certainty that Jane Stanford was murdered and we have a panorama of the evidence for David Starr Jordan's heretofore unimaginable evils, unimaginable perhaps to many of today's readers, but observed day-by-day by many before and after 1905.

In following up Robert Cutler's leads, and Van Dyke's, I have probed a larger truth of these murderous charades. From Cutler's labors we have been prompted to establish a full profile of the fraud.

COLUMN ONE

The Alma Mater Mystery

■ Stanford's cofounder was poisoned, an academic sleuth contends. He suspects its first president of a cover-up — or worse.

By LEE ROMNEY
Times Staff Writer

Who murdered Jane Stanford?

According to the Stanford University archives, nobody. For now, the official version says the sturdy matron who co-founded the university with her husband died of heart failure after a picnic in Honolulu in 1905.

That, says a retired Stanford physician, is a cover-up.

Jane Stanford, concludes Dr. Robert Cutler in a slim volume just published by the university's press, was poisoned with strychnine in the second such attempt on her life in as many months. But someone saw to it that the truth was buried.

Another Stanford professor, writing recently in an academic journal, raises a tantalizing possibility: Could the murderer have been Stanford's revered first president, David Starr Jordan?

The two professors are turning the university's carefully tended mythology upside down.

"A lot of people inherently think Stanford represents something good and great and almost beyond any imaginable reproach," said Stephen Requa, a Stanford alumnus and distant relative of Leland Stanford — the railroad magnate and U.S. senator who founded the Palo Alto university with his wife, Jane.

"Now comes a great evil at the heart of the myth," Requa said. "It's a blemish on the university. It can't just be brushed off."

MARK BOSTER *Los Angeles Ti*

PENSIVE: *Gov. Gray Davis says he is just beginning to think of his next step, but might seek a position with a nonprofit group working on education, the environment or mentoring of young peop*

14 Die on a Day of
Bloodshed in Iraq

Sad but Accepting,
Davis Muse

Los Angeles Times front page article about The Mysterious Death of Jane Stanford by Robert W.P. Cutler, M.D. in which I was quoted..

Chapter II

The "Gangs" at Stanford

Dr Cutler emailed me on June 23, 2003 about a Stanford University website I had come across

> GREAT FIND! I have never seen that website. The "myth" of Mrs. Stanford's death clearly includes your information to Sylvester – almost verbatim from his memo. The "truth" part clearly (to me also) shows Stanford continues to cover it up through its undying worship of Jordan. You need to get this in the last chapter of your book!

Quite obviously, they were worried I might be spreading rumors (or worse) about that Van Dyke information from 1983, which they now termed the "Legend." Indeed, the website reported Sylvester's memorandum almost verbatim.

I venture to say that at that late date, ten years after my Banner International company had been destroyed and had its assets stolen in Utah in 1993, the website was still there because they were worried I would figure out that there were connections between the crimes. It was still there to counter the allegations about the 1905 murder. They were very worried that the truth might be infectious.

Anyway, I hadn't told "the Legend" to anybody else except Peter Sylvester. They were concerned that I, or anybody else that I might have told, would have finally figured out their secrets, including, as Cutler saw, that my great-grandfather Isaac Requa was the obvious second victim – poisoned only a couple of days after Jane Stanford's funeral. There my grandfather would have encountered all the murderers. Isaac was poisoned at lunch at the Pacific Union Club. According to an account of it written by my grandfather, Mark Requa, it was a second attempt on Isaac – the first coinciding with the first one on Jane. Some at Stanford already knew full well that Jane Stanford had indeed been murdered. They just didn't want it made public.

The university website I discovered in 2003 – just before Dr Cutler's book was published – carried a cleverly constructed piece of disinformation on Mrs Stanford's death that was clearly intended to mislead the reader. (Note the juxtaposition of the headlines – "The Legend" versus "The Truth."):

The Death of Jane Stanford: The Legend

"While on vacation in Honolulu, Mrs. Stanford staggered out into the hall of her hotel and announced that she had been poisoned, after which she collapsed and died. The evidence proving that she was poisoned includes a signed statement from an old man who had been a boy at the time of Mrs. Stanford's death. He stated that he had been delivering something to her from a pharmacy and that he had been asked to have it laced with what turned out to be the poison that killed her.

"The primary culprit of the tremendous crime was David Starr Jordan, the founding president of the University! The evidence that supports this theory includes a thank you note from Jordan to some of her relatives for assisting in her untimely death. Jordan also had a motive – the University, under the leadership of Jordan, would receive all of Jane Stanford's remaining wealth upon her death. Mrs. Stanford and Jordan were in dispute about how the University's money should be spent. Jane wanted to build more buildings and Jordan wanted to establish a more prominent faculty.

"Lastly, there was a multifaceted cover-up that supposedly extends even to the current administration. Jordan apparently leaned on the San Francisco Police to obstruct an investigation of what the post mortem physicians, the toxicologist, and the coroner's jury in Honolulu had ruled a murder. The persistent cover-up of the administration that extends to the present is regarded as a face-saving measure.

The Truth:

"In this case, the truth is in the mind of the believer. No one can say for sure what the precise cause of death actually was. Nevertheless, regardless of contradictory theories, the most plausible scenario remains that Jane Stanford's actual cause of death was a natural heart attack."

Hmm ... the "Truth" according to the University: "Jane Stanford died on Feb. 28, 1905, while on vacation in Honolulu. She was 76. An autopsy revealed evidence of heart disease that may have caused a heart attack. The entire community, including Jordan, was deeply saddened by Jane's death."

But all three experienced doctors who attended Mrs Stanford in her death throes, together with the toxicologists and the pathologist who conducted the autopsy, did say exactly what had killed her. No doubts, no equivocation. She had died from Strychnine poisoning. The Coroner's Jury had agreed.

When I conveyed my findings to Dr Cutler he responded with his "Great Find" comment. It was clear to him that the higher echelons at the university were still covering it up to the present day because David Starr Jordan was still worshipped there.

This seemed to be critical. Stanford's exercise in public relations and spin was made with direct reference to the things I had told Sylvester. What else had they been doing? As Cutler stated well, Stanford University did indeed *worship* David Starr Jordan in a very real sense (the same way that the FBI is still worshiping J. Edgar Hoover with their building in his name). For Stanford administration flatfoots, the cult of Jordan, and the whole Stanford founding myth with its revered notion of the university's on-going sanctity and purity, are just like the way some equate God with country, and patriotism with blind, subservient loyalty.

Challenge those myths and – *voila* you get malice.

The methods that David Starr Jordan used to suppress the reality and the truth were the same that Stanford used against me. Jordan viciously slandered the credible medical authorities who attended Mrs Stanford and performed the autopsy and toxicology. A report issued by the executors of Mrs Stanford's estate claimed that her internal organs had subsequently undergone thorough study in Stanford university laboratories and that no strychnine had been found. This acquired the status of a second autopsy, and the case was "closed." The *New York Times* then issued a statement attributed to David Starr Jordan: "A post-mortem examination [at Stanford University] showed that the aorta had been ruptured ... as the result of fatty degeneration of the heart."

The irrefutable fact is that there never was an examination of any internal organs which would physiologically concentrate strychnine at Stanford, or a post-mortem examination. Only one autopsy was possible because, as we Dr. Cutler noted, most of the internal organs had been examined, chopped up, liquefied, chemically tested for strychnine then disposed of in Hawaii. Jane's remains had been buried and nothing but the previously dissected brain and heart (fixed in preservative) were left for Stanford. Had the aorta – the major large vessel carrying blood from the heart – indeed ruptured, the thorax or abdominal cavity would have filled with blood and become apparent to all of the seven doctors present at the Hawaii autopsy when the chest and abdomen were cut open. A first year medical student could not fail to miss it. This wasn't mere spin from Jordan; it was an outrageous lie and a dreadful slur on the professionalism and competence of the Hawaii doctors.

When the heart was dissected and carefully examined at the autopsy in Hawaii, a few insignificant fatty changes were found in the left ventricle, valves and aorta, and some "whitish opaque areas" and "fatty infiltration of the muscle." These are exceedingly common if not the norm for any person of that age. Dr Wood, the pathologist, reported that the organ was not enlarged and "all the valves of the heart and vessels competent." In other words, there was no evidence of a recent coronary thrombosis which may have led to a heart attack, and certainly no sign of any rupture of the aorta. Medical staff at Stanford would have realized just how ridiculous Jordan's statement to the Press was, and the official line was adjusted to the somewhat less egregious lie of death "most probably" due to "chronic myocarditis."

That was the myth and the legend (really, the blatant lie) that has persisted from 1905 to the present. It was a pure hoax perpetuated by Jordan and others using the power and prestige of the University to back them up, along with Roosevelt as President, and to browbeat the public and police. As Cutler documented, Jordan would continue for twenty years to repeatedly and maliciously degrade those doctors. Meanwhile, Dr Waterhouse, a young doctor he bribed in Honolulu in 1905 to write a report stating that there had not been "one characteristic sign of strychnine poisoning," was ostracized by his fellow medical professionals and died penniless in a skid row hotel in San Francisco. Before his death, Dr Waterhouse admitted that he had been directed to write the report having never seen Jane Stanford. Those Jordan had libeled, on the other hand, all led very respected professional careers.

In recent times, as has become more and more evident with the extensive highly adverse actions against me, senior people at

Stanford are still involved in the cover-up. They were especially eager to dismiss and debunk any such allegations I might make in response to their libel campaigns and other actions detailed in my book's chapter sent to Cutler. He found these the *most compelling* things of all, and Stanford clearly recognized that others would also find them compelling if I were to take any initiative to develop them. That, however, was something I had given no thought to whatsoever after meeting Van Dyke in Hawaii back in 1983, nor throughout the following decade and more.

In the front page *Los Angeles Times* article about Cutler's book, with quotes by myself, there were also quotes from another Stanford professor, Bliss Carnochan: "Could the murderer have been Stanford's revered first president, David Starr Jordan?"

The *Times* also wrote:

> A damning piece by another academic sleuth, recently published in the American Scholar, sidles a little closer to an answer. W.B. Carnochan, a Stanford humanities professor emeritus, details Jordan's firing of Julius Goebel – a German professor who was closely allied with Stanford. Stanford was intent on firing Jordan when she died, Carnochan says. The timing of Goebel's firing -- set in motion just days after the first poisoning – suggests that Jordan may have known Stanford's days were numbered.
>
> "He had the motive," Carnochan writes ...
>
> "When you have an institutional story that enshrines David Starr Jordan as a heroic figure and you find out that he seemed to have feet of clay, if not lead, you are bound to wonder whether you have been deluded," Carnochan said, "whether the whole grand story is on very fragile foundations."

To be sure, Stanford University and others were worried from 1983 onward that I was thus a great risk. But I had no clue about any of this. I didn't even start to think about it until I heard all the gross libels about me that Sylvester and other Stanford people were making in 1997 and afterwards, and that they had done starting with the Utah Court Frauds in 1993.

As "the whole grand story is on very fragile foundations," the university appears to have gone to some extraordinary lengths to try to head off and debunk the information I had received in Hawaii in 1983, even putting up a campus website against it. They were making sure those bits of information were made very difficult, or impossible, for me to follow up and further develop. That's especially what the court fraud in Utah did in 1993, to basically confiscate all my assets. They did not want me to expand upon who were, and why those conspirators had murdered Jane Stanford, and then stole her university. It was strange that all the people since 1905 were just not getting it, that the whole motive (with just murdering Jane per se) was indeed that: to steal the whole university once and for all.

So maybe the Stanford folks were not simply panicked because they needed to enshrine Jordan and keep his altar fires at Stanford burning bright, but because they could not afford to have it realized that the University itself was stolen in 1905 – and that it has stayed "stolen" ever since.

As Professor Julius Goebel made clear in his 1904 letters to Jane Stanford – Stanford got stolen by "gangs."

Cutler had first written to me about Professor Carnochan and Professor Goebel in 2001:

> Date: Wed, 12 Dec 2001 14:15:08 -0800
> From: rwpcutler33@yahoo.com
> Subject: Re: Manuscripts Arrived
> To: sherrickrequa@hotmail.com
>
> Dear Stephen:
>
> I was pleased to learn that the manuscripts had arrived. Your final opinion will be of great interest to me. I have sent the manuscript to six people at Stanford – physicians and historians – whose opinions I also will respect, and they will be discrete I'm sure. I learned from one just today that his article on Jordan's treatment of Julius Goebel, which further substantiates Jordan's egregious and perhaps sinister behavior, has been accepted for publication in *American Scholar*. Goebel will have to factor in a screen play, I should think. After you have pondered the manuscript and had a pleasant vacation in Amsterdam, and I have gotten my reviews, we can plan seriously. I appreciate your thoughts on all of this.
>
> Best regards, Robert

By planning "seriously," he meant following up VanDyke and his information, looking into the apparent intrigue against Isaac

Requa, and contemplating a film treatment. Carnochan, through Cutler, would supply the information which, now, indicates just exactly what was so *hot* then about Jane Stanford's murder – Jordan and Bertha Berner. And remains just as hot today. It was indicated by Professor Julius Goebel and his communications with Jane Stanford in 1904-1905. Some excerpts from letters by Professor Goebel to Jane Stanford include these:

> Events, such as the Gilbert affair, which called for concerted action for the purpose of "whitewashing" one of their members brought the [Jordan] "clique" together still closer.... For there are men at this University who are entirely out of place in an institution like ours. They are kept here, as I know on good authority, solely for the purpose of doing the detestable work of detectives among the students and faculty.

As Carnochan has written, Goebel contended that after receiving his letter Mrs. Stanford intended to look into a number of controversial matters more carefully and to reinvestigate the Professor Gilbert sex scandal. The latter, writes Carnochan, "especially seemed to have aroused all the wrath of which, she as a virtuous woman and founder of a co-educational institution, was capable of. These matters had now led her to contemplate the final remedy ... the removal of the President."

Mrs Stanford's secretary, and David Starr Jordan's secret lover, Bertha Berner, had notified Jordan of this right away. Indeed, she had been notifying him of everything, including Jane's feud with Collis Huntington, multi-millionaire, one of the 'Big Four' in railroads in the west and president of the Southern Pacific. In addition to the theft of the university this was possibly a crucial factor in Jane's demise, just as it definitely was in that of her close family friend and fellow murder victim, Isaac Requa. It is most likely that Jordan was in tow with Huntington and with E. H. Harriman. Harriman was a stockbroker who had gained control of the Union Pacific Railroad in 1898 and Huntingdon's Southern Pacific in 1902 with credit from his close associate, J. D. Rockefeller. Determined to gain a total monopoly of all America's great railroads, they set out to grab control of my great-grandfather Isaac Requa's Central Pacific with its 421 locomotives, 8,000 freight cars and thousands of miles of track. Like Harriman, David Starr Jordan was closely linked to Rockefeller, who was pouring millions in to support his work on racist eugenics at Stanford.

Isaac Requa was also the only one with the great wealth and clout to take these conspirators to the mat over Jane's murder, as they no doubt realized when they all attended her funeral. Two days was about as long as they could leave it till Isaac's lunch at the Pacific Union Club was laced with poison.

Professor Goebel had written to Jane Stanford:

> I can describe best by comparing it to the "political rings" and "gangs" of our large cities. Soon after the Ross affair the management considered it advisable to bring together more closely the "faithful ones," so as to forestall possible opposition and revolt in the future.

The Ross affair concerned the firing of Professor Ross, at the insistence of Mrs Stanford, for extreme racist political remarks in public speeches in which he had referred to immigrants, such as the Chinese, as sub-humans. The significance of these factors quoted by Carnochan of Professor Goebel was not immediately apparent, the time frame concerned having been 1905. But this significance would start to become clear after 2010 when a re-invigoration of the original Stanford-based libel campaign against myself began anew while I was in Honduras. I then knew that the Stanford issues had to be got to the bottom of. Many of those conspiring against Jane Stanford or knowledgeable about her poisoning were fanatical eugenicists/racists of the most embarrassingly rabid proportions ever allowed in the public sphere.

David Starr Jordan, President of Stanford University, led the way in 1902, announcing racist/eugenicist principles in publishing *Blood of a Nation* in which he stated that, "The pauper is the victim of heredity, but neither Nature nor Society recognizes that as an excuse for his existence." He could have interchanged (and did many times to come) several other words for pauper that his own unique evolving vocabulary and scientific terminology were producing, such as the unfit, degenerates, the feeble-minded, and those of inferior stock or, as Prof. Eduard Ross of Stanford had also been stating it at that time, the sub-humans for whom neither he nor Jordan believed had available from Nature or Society any excuses for their existence.

Prof. Eduard A. Ross, allied at Stanford with Jordan, was an early supporter of the "Race Suicide" doctrine, and expressed his hatred of other races in strong and crude language in public speeches. Indeed, he objected to Chinese immigrant labor (on both economic and racial grounds). This position was at odds with the university's founding family, the Stanfords, who had made their fortune in Western rail construction – a major employer of Chinese laborers. This was too much for Jane Stanford, who fired him in 1900.

One of the most widely read books on the Race Suicide issue was *The Old World in the New*, by Ross. He believed in the conventional myth of Nordic supremacy and the need for a program of positive eugenics in order to preserve Anglo-Saxon Americanism against pollution through immigration with a chapter showing how "Immigrant Blood" was slowly polluting the purer "American Blood." Obsessed with race, Ross was convinced that "the blood being injected into the veins of our people was sub-human"; the newer immigrants were "morally below the races of northern Europe"; and that it all would end in "Race Suicide." Did he determine in his Stanford laboratory, with or without Jordan, which racial samples of blood were morally below or above any of the others? In any event, Jane Stanford had Ross, a Jordan protégé, fired for these expressed sentiments.

Another key member of the front-line group of conspirators involved in Jane Stanford's murder was Whitelaw Reid. He was owner-publisher of the *New York Tribune*, the largest U.S. newspaper, and the political "voice" of Roosevelt and the Republican Party. Reid was (supposedly) both an Executor of Jane Stanford's Estate and a University Trustee. His father-in-law was also Darius Ogden Mills, formerly California's richest man before Mills' daughter married Reid and they moved to New York City. Reid was a staunch White-Supremacist in no uncertain political and rhetorical terms in his newspaper editorials – also warning in "Race Suicide" jargon of the impending "calamity" from an influx, for example, of Puerto Rican "inferior mixed-race blood." The enemy, he wrote, (the Puerto Rican mixed-breed and half-savages) were at "the gate" ready to "breach the citadel." Thus, when the need to eliminate Jane Stanford arose in 1905 before she could fire Jordan, this circle of virulent racist opportunists closed ranks. Reid exerted his Executor duties immediately to seize all of Jane´s assets, and to secure control with Jordan and Mills. Mills and Reid had arrived all the way from New York City right on cue in California, just as Jane was poisoned in Honolulu.

Meanwhile, Reid had left his editorship and other control positions in others' hands at the *New York Tribune* until he could get back to New York. Securing control of Stanford University and Jane`s personal assets were more important.

President Theodore Roosevelt, an already notorious racist of frequent crude racial epithets, was magnetized by Ross' and Jordan's "Race Suicide" doctrine. TR made Race Suicide into a full-bore Republican political campaign slogan by 1903. He continued to correspond about these matters with Ross long after Ross' firing and was already on close terms with Jordan by 1902 (as seen in letters), when Jordan published his *Blood of a Nation* tract. Jordan had already been pandering for years to large money interests hostile to Jane Stanford (e.g. railroad magnate Collis Huntington, President of Southern Pacific Railroad) with whom both Stanfords had been feuding bitterly and publicly through the 1890s surrounding Central Pacific matters).

Since the firing of Professor Ross in 1900, it may be deemed certain that Jordan was evolving contingency plans to avert, by any means possible, that fate for himself. He thus laid plans, if need be, to eliminate Jane Stanford and to seize full control of the University. There was also the factor of the racist fervor around David Starr Jordan's and Eduard Ross' pseudo-science racist eugenics. A planned push to enact forced sterilization and mixed-race marriage bans legislation was at stake in 27 states, starting most critically in 1905, just as Jane was deciding to fire Jordan. Thus Jane had to go. It was essential to preserve Jordan´s pulpit where his reasons or recognitions (or not) for excuses for existence could simply be declared and promulgated *ex cathedra* by Jordan for the foundations with the big money, and then for Legislators and Legislatures across the country – no questions asked (unless Jordan was fired).

A judgment of Jordan at that time was made by Stanford Professor Julius Goebel, as researched by Carnochan:

> In January 1906, he wrote a letter that referred to [Jane Stanford] as "the good woman whose noble memory I cannot permit to be ... tarnished." Of Jordan he wrote, "this man is loathed and despised not only by his students and professors but practically by the whole academic world."

As I have written, there is media potential in such a well-documented human monster as David Starr Jordan. One of these aspects was covered by the first copyrighted treatment in 2004. It concerned the Gilbert Affair:

> In 1901, the zoologist Charles Henry Gilbert, who had studied with Jordan at Indiana and was now one of his close associates – had been charged with carrying on an improper relationship with a young woman working at the library. Jordan, in Goebel's account, had bullied an "innocent young man" (then an assistant librarian, and a Stanford graduate) who blew the whistle on Gilbert, threatening him with "incarceration in the insane asylum for sexual perversity … if he did not leave California at once." Though the press got hold of the allegations, Jordan and his supporters were apparently successful in performing the "whitewashing" to which Goebel refers [in letters to Jane Stanford].

Per Carnochan, Goebel contended that Mrs. Stanford intended to look into a number of controversial matters more carefully and to reinvestigate the Gilbert scandal. The latter, especially, seemed to have aroused her wrath. These matters had led her to contemplate "the final remedy … the removal of the President."

In sum, to insure Jordan's tenure as a stooge of higher interests, what actually precipitated Jane Stanford's murder was an emergency: her threat to remove Jordan over a sex scandal involving his cohort Professor Gilbert, who may have also been able to blackmail Jordan by disclosing his affair with Bertha Berner and that Jordan was paying her to spy on Jane Stanford. The clincher evidence is in a letter Professor Goebel wrote to Stanford Trustee Horace Davis in 1907 after he had moved on to Harvard.

The letter implies that Jordan was capable of doing whatever he needed to do: "He knew that this investigation [of the Gilbert affair] would result in the exposure of Gilbert as well as of himself and of his coterie, and he made up his mind that it had to be prevented at any price."

Horace Davis confirmed these matters also, in a letter in 1907 to Edmund James, President of the University of Illinois:

> Davis wrote James again, adding details about Gilbert and his "improper conduct toward one of the girls in the University Library.…

Dr. Goebel was unfortunately an eye-witness to some of these questionable incidents and strenuous efforts were made to induce him to declare publicly that he believed the accusation was groundless; but this he refused to do, and this refusal caused "permanent coldness between Goebel and the President's intimates."

As noted earlier Julius Goebel wrote about the "ops" on campus. "For there are men at this University who are entirely out of place in an institution like ours. They are kept here ... solely for the purpose of doing the detestable work of detectives among the students and faculty."

The Stanford campus was under surveillance. These "gangs" were professionals, in the same way CIA agents are today. Could the murder of Jane Stanford have been a well-planned contingency to insure a horrific elite eugenics agenda? With Jordan as a proponent and Stanford University as his necessary pulpit? It would also give behind-the-scenes long-term control of Stanford University. That's about how it stacks up.

The killing of Jane Stanford is perhaps the first demonstrable "coup" engineered by a U.S. President via murder. Taking over and maintaining Stanford University as a cornerstone and powerhouse for the New World Order, along with the Rockefeller Foundation may explain much surrounding the murder of Jane Stanford and the crimes against Banner International and myself.

The Rockefellers and their cohorts at Stanford have been worried that the reality of the elite crime syndicate from 1905 to the present will be revealed – with its long-term objective for worldwide fascism under the control of their bankers.

The world must know that since February 28, 1905 Stanford University has been a stolen "asset" for the most-wicked. Let the faculty, alumni, and students reclaim it in memory of their murdered Jane Stanford.

Chapter III

The Great Evil at the Heart of the Myth

I could see in 1993 that the Stanford administration was really worried about something. The Stanford police chief, as I found out through calls made by London investigators later in 1997, had even sent out notices to faculty members in 1993 – coinciding with the Utah receivership frauds against my Banner International company – about my posing some sort of a risk, a physical risk, to faculty members. It was surreal. My mailbox on campus was also closed down without any notice at the time of the receivership actions in Utah. They didn't want me to receive the notice served on those court actions. Organized crime is all about criminals being able to utilize government agencies to channel their crimes. I discovered the truth of this during 1993, and detailed much of it in my book published in 2009. *The Great American Gold Grab*, was basically a 650-page affidavit on all those events. I had to detail everything I could think of while my memory was still fresh.

At the time in 1993 I could imagine no direct connection between Stanford and the Utah court frauds. But with the materialization of Dr. Cutler in 2001 with the internal Stanford University Sylvester Memorandum he had found in university archives on my learning in 1983 about Jordan's and Mills' involvement in Jane Stanford's demise, there appeared to be some connection between the bizarre events at Stanford and the Utah actions.

The takeover gang in Utah in 1993 had instigated the court actions and completed them within a 24-hour period – before the notice of them was even mailed to my already shut-down post office box. The instigators had very good reason for not wanting me to know about these actions for as long as possible.

Somebody at the Stanford Post Office (a branch of the U.S. Post Office) apparently took care of my mailbox, closing it without authorization.

Hidden forces burst into the open with the 1993 Utah receivership frauds. These transpired literally overnight without any notice and proceeded with the destruction of Banner International and the stripping and scavenging of all its assets by a corrupt receiver.

As my attorney, Dr. William Pepper, had assessed after I retained him in London in 1999, the receivership action had been baseless, with no legitimate legal rationale. The company had no material debt. All its essential obligations were paid a year in advance. We had $400,000 in the checking accounts; and we were verging on great success in discovering major new gold deposits near Ely, Nevada and north of Elko.

But, as I came to discover, the Stanford connection was much wider, deeper, and more complex than the superficial facts might suggest. There were many Stanford names on the Banner mailing list, including several professors. Initially, I had thought that they might have just been implicated in Vancouver and San Francisco securities rackets and that they were using their combined influence to create a smear campaign against me as a way of keeping me occupied and not able to expose it all. That seemed at the time the simplest and most obvious explanation. But, as would become apparent, that barely scratches the surface of what was going on.

I had also distributed in June 1993 packets of information on the crimes in progress against my company to all the Stanford Law and Earth Sciences professors. Surely, I thought, some of those people could see that organized criminal activities were in progress and that Stanford people were implicated, even if only passively and without their being aware of it, in a substantial securities racket. I was therefore under the gross illusion that a great institution like Stanford University might actually be interested in rooting out some of its bad seeds. But as I found out, almost no one is ever interested in voluntarily rooting out anything. Rarely does anyone expose their own dirt – or anybody else's – until forced to, like the Catholic Church over its child-molestation scandals. Things almost always remain covered up until the bitter end – especially with powerful institutions, and that includes the federal government.

We can only wonder when and what the "bitter end" for the federal government might be when it is eventually forced to come to terms with the vast depth and breadth of its corruption, going back at least to the 1963 assassination of John Kennedy, along with its decades of denial and cover-up.

But in 1993 it never occurred to me that Stanford might be worried about something very much worse than stock-exchange racketeering, and that because of that, they may have found some great incentive to see me and my company permanently destroyed. That "something very much worse" turned out, in the first instance, to be how and why Jane Stanford was murdered and by whom, more than 88 years earlier.

My first indication of this came in 1997 in London when I prompted London media people to make calls on campus to those who had been on Banner's mailing list. One of them was Peter Sylvester. In 1983, he had been an official in the Office of Development, the university's fund raising office (and he would still be there in 1993). I had met Peter through my Banner company's director and a geologist friend Joe Ash.

One of the reasons I got them to call Sylvester, besides his being on the mailing list, was because of his ties with Ash, who had lived in his house as an undergraduate. I used to see Sylvester once in a while around the campus or in Palo Alto and before that at his home with Ash. I had seen him right after I had spoken with the Hawaiian historian Robert Van Dyke in 1983, and related to him Van Dyke's comments about Jane Stanford's 1905 murder and his compiled evidence on David Starr Jordan's and Darius Ogden Mills' alleged implication in it.

Sylvester's first reaction back in 1983 was to say to me, "Great, just in time to kick off the Centennial" – alluding to the big drive to raise hundreds of millions of dollars for Stanford to mark the 100th anniversary of its founding. Sylvester was seemingly quite concerned that such disclosures as Jane Stanford's murder with the founding university President's role in it could adversely impact his fund-raising programs.

I would, however, scarcely give a thought about the issue of Jane Stanford's murder until fourteen years later, when the London media people called Sylvester in 1997, and he launched into a phenomenal diatribe about me. He said that I was "in trouble" with my family and that I was "something of a playboy in Hawaii" who had "squandered" Banner's money (as I heard Sylvester say on speaker-phone when the media people called him).

When the media people weren't buying Peter's rap very readily, he suddenly grasped at more straws: "Oh, yes," he said, I was "obsessed" with the murder of Mrs. Stanford by David Starr Jordan, and I was "going around trying to prove it" and was "off-center" about it. He then added that even if it were true that Jordan had killed Mrs. Stanford, it "didn't make any difference – not now, not at this point."

But that was not true. Stanford is still under the sway, as we shall see, of the same *interests* who had murdered Jane Stanford to get that control. They had to kill her before she could fire David Starr Jordan as university President, and they had to move quickly. That's what prompted the rushed train trips to California for Darius Ogden Mills and his son-in-law, Whitelaw Reid, to get there in time to cover her murder up along with Jordan.

In any case, Sylvester apparently knew the complete party line of smear by the Utah court fraudsters, and he employed it as though the contents of his accusations were a matter of personal knowledge. He also added that the interviewer would "love" Phillip Fay Stevenson's op-ed letters to the San Francisco newspapers. Apparently, Peter wanted to get some PR in for Stevenson, who was nothing more than a cocktail hour chatter-box on the phone with people he was trying to get involved in his Vancouver securities rackets to defraud Banner. So Sylvester needed to put in a good word in PR for him *for some reason*.

Then I asked the London filmmakers to call Dr. George Thompson, a geophysics professor and Dean of the Geophysics Department at Stanford who had also been on the mailing list. He was a friend of Dr. Dennis Burke years before when Burke had mapped our Merritt Mountain gold property. Thompson first said that he remembered me back in the 1980s, when I "was sane." Then, in a mind-boggling stroke of denial, he said that I had never even been a Stanford student. That was something which would come as a big surprise to the university registrar.

Thompson was also quite eager to discount the reality that the Nevada properties could shape up into mines, stating that there was just "a little bit of mineralization" there, which most likely wouldn't make a mine. According to all the geologists who had seen it, however, the mineralization was widespread on both properties. $150 million in placer gold in 2008 values, *one of the biggest placer amounts in Nevada history*, had been taken out of Osceola. Thompson had never even been to either of the properties and knew absolutely nothing about them, but he was willing to posture with his Ph.D. credentials from his Stanford office as though he did. He questioned whether what I had found at the Nevada properties was just all "in Steve Requa's mind." He was quite friendly and even affable as he made these outrageous statements, and appeared casual and comfortable with what he was saying.

Professor Thompson also added that the Stanford Police Chief, Marv Harrington, had circulated a memo to faculty advising them that I was to be considered dangerous – a possible threat to the safety of the faculty – and the faculty ought to know. That undoubtedly explained some disturbing things that happened to me during a visit to the university in October 1993. Professor Kincheloe, a shareholder in my Banner International Company, appeared to have been alerted to my presence on campus and was inexplicably nervous in my presence. I now finally understood the very uncomfortable feeling I experienced that day that I was being followed and constantly under surveillance as I moved around campus. It wasn't my imagination. It happened – just as I had thought!

When the filmmakers next called Chief Harrington at the campus police station, he refused to comment, aside from saying that he knew who I was, and referred them to the Stanford press office. As Thompson quoted him, Harrington had written in his memo to faculty that "this guy [me] is not wired correctly," and that if I showed up, the police should be contacted immediately. So it had been reported to Kincheloe and many others that I was to be considered dangerous. Sadly, good people at Stanford who knew me bought into the charade that I was "crazy, armed and dangerous."

So by this time (in 1997) I was just beginning to realize how deep the intrigue had been at Stanford – as if I hadn't had a complete demonstration of it in October 1993 during the Utah court frauds.

* * * * *

Of critical interest and importance at Stanford was the presence of a letter of recommendation written for me by geologist Roger Bowers in the early 1990s. The letter was kept in my personal file at the university's job placement center. By 1997 the party line being spouted was that the Nevada properties had "no value," and that very little had been spent on gathering data on them, when in fact over $2 million had been spent from 1973 to 1993. Therefore, it would be very inconvenient if Bowers' 1991 recommendation letter on file at Stanford extolling my Osceola work and its very great value was still on file at Stanford's Placement Center. In that letter, Bowers had written about how I had personally solved the Osceola Mother Lode riddle, and that I had found where the lode was and had done *by myself* what large mining companies with big staffs very seldom accomplish. This letter also stated how valuable the Requa/Hoover Files were and that the company was well-poised for great success on several fronts. All of this was quite true, if suddenly inconvenient.

Needless to say, I was therefore then very interested in what had happened to that letter. Not only was its praise of me in contradiction to the "crackpot" image that was currently being espoused, but the letter's admission that I had found the mother lode, and its statements of the value of the files and the findings, were completely at odds with all the fictions of the takeover group and their securities racketeers who were stealing all Banner's assets.

In sum, any evidence for my accomplishments in Nevada and later in Honduras had to be eliminated. The obvious plan was for Bowers himself to be "finding" the Osceola "mother lode," the same mother lode that his 1991 Stanford Placement Center letter had praised me for already having found. But they would have to get me out of the way first, one way or another.

Sure enough, when I asked the film people to call the Stanford Placement Center and ask about the contents of my file, all my recommendation letters were there except the one from Bowers. Among the letters remaining were recommendations from professors in the Earth Sciences Department under whom I had studied, praising my demonstrated geological capabilities; and one from Henry Hunt Keith, a professor at the Business School of San Francisco State University, who had introduced me to Carlos Rodriguez-Pastor, the former Finance Minister of Peru. Professor Keith wrote that I was one of the most capable entrepreneurs he had ever known. All these letters were significant factors in my success; during the 1987–1992 period I would have the Stanford Placement Center send them out to potential investors, just as they do on behalf of job applicants. Bowers letter from 1991, however, had conspicuously disappeared.

Stanford, it seems, had done someone a favor by covertly removing Bowers' letter from my file (attesting as it did to the great prospective worth of Banner's assets). I was naturally getting pretty upset about this and about Stanford's emerging role in facilitating such frauds.

The university had told me nothing about removing the letter, either before or after the fact. When I inquired about it in 1997, they just said the letter wasn't there. Under continuing pressure from me, it would take *four years* for them to fess up. In 2001, after I started lobbying the Faculty Senate members *en masse* by email, the university counsel Debra Zumwalt *finally* stated that Bowers had asked them to remove it, and that they were obliged to do so. But they still wouldn't answer why they hadn't told me about it at the time, nor why it took four years of heated pressure on them before they admitted that they had removed it.

From all of this, I therefore began to suspect that one reason for Sylvester portraying me as being "obsessed" about Mrs. Stanford's murder was to destroy my credibility and to portray me as a "conspiracy theorist." That was clear enough in Sylvester's chats with London media people. In any case, back in 1983 the concern had been about the effect the reported evidence for Jane Stanford's murder might have on the Centennial fund-raising campaign.

What it all seemed to come down to at the time was that I knew too much, that I could not be depended upon to keep quiet about it all. Their best insurance against this was to discredit me and confiscate my assets. As a part of this agenda in both California and Utah, Sylvester could pitch the idea that I was trying to embarrass the university by attempting to prove that Jordan had murdered Jane Stanford – making me *ipso facto* a crackpot.

But as I was to see years later, the uppermost university echelon, including Sylvester, already knew full well that Jane Stanford had indeed been murdered. They just didn't want it made public. Of course, Sylvester knew their accusation that I was "going around" being "obsessed" about it was bogus; but he really did not like the idea of me knowing about it per se. Why could that have been?

* * * * *

In 2000, I had William Pepper call Stanford University's General Counsel, Ms. Debra Zumwalt, about security files the university was keeping on me. Ms. Zumwalt did not know, of course, that the London filmmakers had tape recordings of four Stanford officials talking about these files. Pepper later, on September 28, 2001, described this in a memo:

> She categorically advised me that there was no security file being kept on you at Stanford. She also denied that there was any effort being made to harm you or prejudice your interests.... In a subsequent conversation, she advised me that she had spoken to the University security officials and that they had confirmed her initial information that no security file on you was being kept.

Ms. Zumwalt's reported statements, in light of the four recordings of Stanford people, were therefore all gross fictions – either blatant lies or indications of the most amazing cluelessness and incompetence. At least a professor, the campus police chief, a fund-raiser, and the alumni director had all spoken about their knowledge of the matter and the files that the police were saying they were keeping on me in 1993 – "before Requa went to England," as Thompson had said. With whom could Ms. Zumwalt have "checked" to determine that Stanford kept no security files on me? Evidently, she didn't check with the police chief. In those conversations with Pepper, Ms. Zumwalt also made the requisite party-line references to Pepper that questioned my "mental stability" and "credibility." She added that my emails to faculty members about the situation were "a nuisance," and that they were "not taken seriously and quickly thrown away."

Nonetheless, I had succeeded, at least with some Stanford people, in countering the Stanford juggernaut of smear tactics. Sometime later, after issues surrounding Jane Stanford's murder and Dr. Cutler emerged in context with the Banner ones, I would get the following email from a professor who stated:

> I have been following your emails to the [University] President. I'm not sure why you have copied the department but I have been encouraged to see someone stand up for truth and to hold the administration accountable. I am advocating for you and respect the courage it takes to stand up to the administration. It is apparent Stanford has lacked integrity in multiple areas and I hope your case is a lightning bolt

that illuminates the cover up. Whatever happened to the commitment to truth? I'm very disappointed by the indignities you have had to suffer. All the best.

One possible reason the takeover charlatans were so confident in their depredations of Banner International might have been because they had Stanford University on hand to remove Bowers' letter, had its police chief to defame and discredit me, and were able to posture and spread the sorts of libelous things Ms. Zumwalt was still doing in 2000. Stanford was decisively and pro-actively on the side of Bowers and his employers. It would take me until 2004 – after a steady stream of communications over a two- year period with Dr. Robert Cutler to appreciate these facts. This period culminated in the publication by Stanford University Press of his book *The Mysterious Death of Jane Stanford*. The announcement of the book appeared on the Stanford Press website in 2003 as follows:

> Jane Stanford, the co-founder of Stanford University, died in Honolulu in 1905, shortly after surviving strychnine poisoning in San Francisco. The inquest testimony of the physicians who attended her death in Hawaii led to a coroner's jury verdict of murder – by strychnine poisoning.
>
> Stanford University President David Starr Jordan promptly issued a press release claiming that Mrs. Stanford had died of heart disease, a claim that he supported by challenging the skills and judgment of the Honolulu physicians and toxicologist. Jordan's diagnosis was largely accepted and promulgated in many subsequent historical accounts.
>
> In this book, the author reviews the medical reports in detail to refute Dr. Jordan's claim and to show that Mrs. Stanford indeed died of strychnine poisoning. His research reveals that the professionals who were denounced by Dr. Jordan enjoyed honorable and distinguished careers. He concludes that Dr. Jordan went to great lengths, over a period of nearly two decades, to cover up the real circumstances of Mrs. Stanford's death.

The *Stanford Alumni* magazine in a lengthy feature article and review of Cutler's book wrote the following:

> Who Killed Jane Stanford?
>
> New investigations confirm she was poisoned by strychnine.... Someone got away with murder.... Speculating on

an unsolved, century-old murder is risky business – something serious scholars tend to shy away from, except, perhaps, when they speak off the record. But for the record, Cutler effectively makes this case: Jane Stanford did not die a natural death.

As Cutler documented, David Starr Jordan went to great lengths over a period of twenty years to suppress these facts and to discredit and maliciously defame those who had established them. His position and his official actions as President of the university were enough to suppress a murder investigation. The person with the biggest obvious motive for the murder and who had the most to benefit from Mrs. Stanford's death was Jordan himself, whom Mrs. Stanford had been preparing to dismiss at the time of her murder. Evidence Cutler provided also shows that Jordan had foreknowledge that Mrs. Stanford's days were numbered. He was preparing just before her death to fire one of her most trusted faculty allies, Professor Julius Goebel. This goal would have been impossible to fulfill if she had stayed alive.

Over the next two months, the reporting on Cutler's book mushroomed. First, it was a front-page story in the *San Jose Mercury News,* the third-largest-circulation newspaper in California. That article arose from an email campaign I made to Stanford professors about the murder and the relationship of its ongoing cover-up to Stanford's evident hostilities against me. One of the faculty who got my email sent it to the newspaper. One of their reporters then contacted me and interviewed Cutler. The newspaper also quoted my comments about it being appropriate for the university now to strip Jordan's name from various buildings and memorials on campus. But cults die hard. As a case in point, the FBI building in Washington *still* bears J. Edgar Hoover's name, and after all the world has been fully appraised of his grotesque realities.

A *Los Angeles Times* reporter based in San Francisco, Lee Romney, saw that article. She interviewed me by phone while I was in Holland, and wrote a more in-depth piece in which I was quoted at the beginning of the article. A quoted comment was, "Now comes a great evil from the heart of the myth." This article was printed on the front page of the *Los Angeles Times* on October 10, 2003, and my quote ended up in other newspapers as the article was syndicated across the country.

Up until 2003, I had thought the whole Stanford drama around me from 1993 onward had taken place simply because some rich

Stanford donors, or some potential Stanford donors, possibly needed me identified as a threat to the continuing influx of the university's donations from them (aside from their convenient allegation that I was a danger to the public safety of its faculty). As I have found, when the very rich want to pull a major crime they often rely on philanthropy to give them a good cover and to get the recipients of their largesse (perhaps like Stanford University) to do whatever is needed – and those beneficiaries will fall all over themselves to do what they just *think* might be wanted of them.

But, perhaps much more importantly, I figured out eventually that there was indeed the basis for an authentic U.S. national security operation here – warped and corrupt though it was. I had long ascertained that one very real issue was the control of the developing mineral wealth and gold of Central America, and in many of the new gold mines yet to be discovered there and in the western U.S. That – as former Peruvian Finance Minister Carlos Rodriguez-Pastor had told Alberto Fujimori in my presence – is what was "muy importante." The right-wing political factions and their national security proponents, whether in the FBI or CIA or in Guatemala, Honduras, and the U.S. would want to make sure those gold mines were going to be in their hands (especially perhaps so that some of South America's dirty cocaine money could be laundered through the mining operations). William Pepper had alluded to some of these involved realities in the video interview in 1999:

> If you're not in the club you know you're an outsider and
> then you're dangerous … ultimately you've got to be killed.
> If that's the only way they can stop you, they will kill you.

Not wanting to be in the club, and very much wanting to keep control of your big assets – resources like gold and oil – is one way you get to be a "national security" threat, and can be enough to get you killed. It can also be enough to get some right-wing criminals to contrive a "national security" issue with false reporting to the FBI (such as had definitely been done against me), falsification of FBI records by criminalized FBI agents to allege "radical" ties, and prompting naïve FBI agents to then participate in illegal hostilities. The latter is also surely what was happening with Banner International, although in Banner's case the hostilities and the smear campaign were also coming from the top of the FBI, as FBI Agent Mike Christman in Utah told me in 1993.

Stanford, regarding Banner International, may have become essential in the "national security" game. Consider that, in 2004, eight of the thirty-one individuals seated on the Pentagon's Defense Policy Board were Fellows from Stanford's Hoover Institution, a conservative think tank that gets much criticism from other Stanford faculty for its doctrinaire, right-wing Republican mentality. Many members of that board also have close ties to defense contractors who could benefit economically from the information they get at these Pentagon board meetings.

George W. Bush's former National Security Advisor and subsequent Secretary of State Condoleezza Rice, besides being a Hoover Senior Fellow, was also a Chevron Director. The Hoover Institution and Stanford provide the credentials, the elite institutional backdrop, and the proper academic rationale and obfuscating rhetoric for much of the right-wing and defense-establishment political agenda – especially for their wars for profit.

Many of the Hoover Fellows (and certainly Rice in the Bush II administration) provide essential validation for contrived wars and other policies, complete with palatable-sounding academic and scientific jargon. They and the Hoover Institution are, in essence, academic prostitutes, and much of the Stanford academic community realizes this.

Stanford University pays the bills of the Hoover Institution and places many of Hoover's Fellows into faculty positions. Anything that would seriously undermine Stanford's credibility, its mythology, its finances, or its image and reputation would thus be a *big* negative to the Hoover Institution. Any threat to the Hoover Institution would be considered, in effect, a threat to "national security." Without my knowing it, I had perhaps started to pose this threat to them in 1983 after my trip to Hawaii and after Sylvester wrote his internal university memos to Stanford administrators informing them that I had learned that Jordan and Darius Ogden Mills were being alleged, *with new evidence*, to be behind Jane Stanford's murder.

Following the flurry of front-page reporting on the Stanford murder exposures, I received an email from Dr. Pepper as follows:

Dear Stephen,

First of all let me commend you on the work you have done with respect to the death of Mrs Stanford. It is clear to me that you have opened a can of worms and set out a very credible case of apparent murder based upon the Cutler evidence. Your diligence serves well the Stanford family and, although they do not realize it at this time, the entire Stanford community. Of course, I can only urge you to follow through with this work. There is, as you know, no statute of limitations involving murder. I have no doubt that it is a potentially very worrying matter for the university.
As ever,

W.F. Pepper

That the university was indeed very worried was soon evident in the continuing newspaper coverage. On October 23, 2003, Tania Rojas wrote an article in the *Stanford Daily* that included the following:

On the evening of Feb. 28, 1905, Jane Stanford asked her personal secretary for a glass of bicarbonate soda. Into the night, servants heard her agonizing cry: "I think I have been poisoned..." Minutes later, Jane Stanford was pronounced dead.

Whodunit?

That's the question posed by retired Stanford physician Robert Cutler in his book, *The Mysterious Death of Jane Stanford*. The book has piqued the attention of the national media with a provocative claim: Contrary to the University's official story – that Jane died of heart failure – she was actually poisoned in the Moana Hotel in Hawaii, and her death was covered up by then-University President David Starr Jordan.

"The 'Stanford community,' as you call it, has been quick to say that all scrutiny is welcome," said Leora Romney, a *Los Angeles Times* reporter who wrote a front- page feature on the book's claim. "But at the same time, there is great reluctance to acknowledge that Starr Jordan may have had less than honorable motives. Cutler's research is solid. His scholarship has not been challenged. So why not accept his conclusions? The University insists on stopping short of that."

Jordan perjured the public by saying she had died of heart disease. That story has been kept on official records ever since. However, according to Cutler, Jordan knew of the reality of the poisoning but denied it and continued to do so publicly. In his book, Cutler details Jordan's cover-ups in criminal disparagement of the doctors and coroner's jury who had the irrefutable evidence she was murdered.

Both the successor of Stanford Vice President Freelan, Gordon Earle, and the university's Chairman of the Board of Trustees, Isaac Stein, commented that Cutler had "proved nothing." They were, of course, not willing to take Cutler to task on any of the medical facts. As the *Los Angeles Times* noted in its front page article on October 10, 2003, everyone else was viewing Cutler's case as medically and historically "irrefutable." But the Stanford administration was saying that Cutler's case for murder was "highly speculative." If ever there was a solid medical case for poisoning, however – one that had nothing at all speculative about it – this was it. The Hawaii Coroner's Jury in 1905 had ruled the same way. But Earle, their good spinmeister, was quoted in the California newspapers as saying the following:

"Some have made the case that President Jordan was involved in a cover-up surrounding the circumstances of Jane Stanford's death.... The University believes that this conclusion is highly speculative and not supported by any solid proof. And there is absolutely no evidence that President Jordan was directly connected in any way in Jane Stanford's death."

Earle and Stein were being true believers in the Stanford cult, but they were also worried about something more palpable and threatening. Along this line I noted that Cutler had found a letter from Jordan to Stanford Board Chairman Samuel Leib. The following appeared in the front-page lead-column article in the *Los Angeles Times* on October 10, 2003:

> Many of the documents and press clippings that Cutler relied on have been sitting in Stanford's archives since the late 1960s.
>
> His first help came from Karen Bartholomew, a board member of the Stanford Historical Society who had written about the death for an in-house publication. In her file: a 12-point letter from Jordan to board of trustees President Samuel F. Leib that suggests he choose whichever alternative to poisoning he thinks most suitable.

"If the tonic theory of strychnine is not acceptable, you have the other, that it was put in by the doctor to bolster up his case, after he had had time to read up on the symptoms a little ... [he is] a man without professional or personal standing," Jordan wrote.

"That was the defining moment," Cutler said of his souring sentiment toward Jordan. "To finger the doctor who had worked all night to help her as having done this himself – that ain't playing around."

But when Cutler obtained the autopsy report and coroner's inquest, he was all the more stunned. "There's nothing more characteristic than strychnine poisoning, nor is there confusion between strychnine poisoning and heart disease," said the neurologist. "It would have been clear to anybody."

On Jordan's hired physician, Dr. Waterhouse, the article stated:

Cutler not only picked apart the medical documents, but also took pains to investigate the reputations of the physicians in Hawaii. All had respectable careers – all save Waterhouse.

Jordan's recruit abandoned his medical practice to invest in Far East rubber plantations, and, after a stint as a clothing salesman, ended up destitute on the streets of San Francisco's Tenderloin district. He died at Stanford Medical School's teaching hospital.

About Jordan's foreknowledge it stated:

A damning piece by another academic sleuth, recently published in the *American Scholar*, sidles a little closer to an answer. W.B. Carnochan, a Stanford humanities professor emeritus, details Jordan's firing of Julius Goebel – a German professor who was closely allied with Stanford. Stanford was intent on firing Jordan when she died, Carnochan says. The timing of Goebel's firing – set in motion just days after the first poisoning – suggests that Jordan may have known Stanford's days were numbered.

So, when Earle said "there is absolutely no evidence that President Jordan was directly connected in any way in Jane Stanford's death," he evades the fact that not only did Jordan have a certain motive – to keep his job – but that his own actions betray his knowledge that her death was imminent. The *Los Angeles Times* article concluded as follows:

> But Gordon Earle, Stanford's vice president of communications, adds that Jordan's legacy remains a strong one.
>
> "When you look at the entirety of President Jordan's career at Stanford, it is clear that he was one of our finest presidents," Earle said. "He deserves to be remembered – and memorialized."
>
> Does it even matter? To some, nothing short of the Stanford mythology is at stake.

In the context of the tissue-paper-thin denials by Earle and Stein, Pepper's comment about there being no statute of limitations for murder set me to thinking. All the people involved in the murder were, of course, dead. But Stanford University itself was thriving, and I wondered about the university's exposure *as an institution*. Could the University itself have been made culpable? Had Jordan irremediably implicated the University *institutionally* in the crime? I thus began suspecting that this was perhaps a factor that had so concerned Sylvester and the administration officials in 1983 and ever since.

It is a question that is worthy of address in view of the extraordinary hostile actions of Stanford University against my person and reputation. It is also worth asking in context of the falsehoods issued by Stanford counsel and vice president, Ms. Zumwalt. Were those falsehoods merely knee-jerk, or were they made knowledgeably? In the context of her efforts to cast aspersions on my sanity to William Pepper, I would tend to suspect that they were knowledgeable lies. Will they be capable of providing a credible reply? I would certainly like to see someone subpoenaed to testify at the hoped-for (and critically required) Congressional investigations into these matters.

With these things in mind, I then took another look at Sylvester's 1983 memo to Freelan and noticed something that had not occurred to me before. As noted earlier, Stanford in public was claiming that there was no reason to conclude Mrs. Stanford had been poisoned. But, as we have already seen, in Sylvester's memo to Freelan, in the very first sentence he straightaway refers to "the

2/28/05 poisoning of Jane Stanford." He didn't say an "alleged" poisoning or a "highly speculative" one. He called it just *the* 2/28/05 poisoning." He appears to be taking the murder for granted, and he apparently knew Freelan was also taking it for granted. Was it common knowledge? Did they all know Stanford's dark, dirty secret already? What Sylvester *was* concerned about in his memo was "something new" that Van Dyke might have come up with to finger Jordan.

During the 2003 syndication of the article in newspapers across the country that followed, I noticed some other interesting discrepancies. One was that Stanford had alleged – in a newspaper headline in 1905 – that "no poison" had been found in Mrs Stanford's organs in Stanford's own labs. But, as we have previously shown, the organs had been chopped up and liquefied for tests in Honolulu, then discarded there. The newspaper headlines about them were planned deceptions and complete fictions put out by Stanford. Stanford was controlling/lying to the press.

Some conclusions therefore seemed rather certain to me. Several people at Stanford already knew in 1905 that Jane Stanford had been murdered. In addition to Jordan, these certainly included the Chairman of the Board and other Trustees. They knew that Jordan was putting out a barrage of deception. Samuel Leib (then Stanford Board Chairman) was advising Jordan. The Trustees were a party to this action. Some, certainly Jordan, knew before the fact that Jane wasn't going to be around much longer. If all these other people knew Jane had been murdered, who were they thinking had done it? They *all* had participated in it one way or another. De facto, it was a coup, in which forces seized control of the university from Jane Stanford.

I must therefore say that I am persuaded that Stanford University – as an institution – would seem to have at least the appearance of culpability in Mrs. Stanford's murder and its cover-up; that the upper echelons of the Stanford administration have known it from 1905 to this day.

But there was still another related area of possible university culpability that would take me a few more months to recognize–relating to me personally and to more of its dark history that was emerging.

The university with all its resourcefulness may have ascertained that I was a legitimate potential heir of the last of the Stanfords – Helen Winslow Stanford, daughter of my grandmother's sister Alice Herrick Stanford. Helen was my father's first cousin. They were a tight family, constantly going back and forth to each other's estates for weeks and months on end. I was also in fact an heir to another of my grandmother's and Alice Stanford's sisters, Margaret Cox Herrick, as was my father. Childless, Helen left her money to Stanford. Would she have done so if she had known that Jane was murdered and that the university as an institution was perhaps implicated in her murder? She would probably have left her fortune instead to family members, as her mother's sister had. I, and other family members, would thus have standing in a civil action to sue the university to recover those funds for the family members. The key fact, however, was simply that I would have had some *legal standing to act* – just to bring all of this out into the open in court.

It went well beyond one possible bequest. If Stanford University was sued, it would cause an upheaval in university politics and control. They would no longer be able to disperse Stanford holy water. Their prized mythology would collapse. "The great evil at the heart of the Stanford myths" would emerge. The heart of Stanford University was black. Legal actions against Stanford, successful or not, of merit or not, could be catastrophic ... there is no statute of limitations on murder.

And then there was (and continues to be) the very real National Security establishment presence at the Hoover Institution There are still (to me) some very big questions that have not been resolved to this day. Why did an "FBI Agent X," as revealed in my previous book, *The Great American Gold Grab*, have a Utah Corporations office records falsification scheme all concocted and ready to go when I arrived in Utah in the spring of 1993? Who really got Stanford to lift the Bowers letter?

The ultimate question, at least as far as Banner was concerned, also remains unresolved: Where are the priceless Requa/Hoover Files?

* * * *

In 2004 I had been hard at work in consultation with Dr. Cutler on a film treatment for the Jane Stanford murder case. He and I had been exchanging emails about it for two years and were focusing on some good ideas for a dramatization of the events. As it turned out, it would be much more dramatic than we expected. Cutler's book had mostly been a research and academic book by a physician into the historical and medical records that had been suppressed. Both Jordan at the time and Stanford University right up to the present had fabricated many myths, and outright lies, to support that suppression. Today they would be criminally chargeable as obstructions of justice, at least. After the publicity flurry in the newspapers, I could see that the Stanford issue was going to be a part of my salvation by helping to restore my credibility, which university people had tried systematically to destroy. Very damning for Stanford would be its heinous acts, now coming to light, to discredit the autopsy doctors – in 1905 and for 20 years thereafter – and then, nearly a century later, employing similar tactics to try to destroy me.

For those two and a half years, Dr. Cutler and I corresponded several times a week. I sent him my book installments as I wrote them, and he was extremely perceptive and supportive. His wisdom and personality seemed to envelop my thinking for those years. He was an extraordinarily kind soul of both brilliance and modesty, with an ability to see through sham right away. He especially enjoyed my characterizations of the San Francisco socialites.

In February 2004, Dr. Cutler sent me a very detailed timeline for the murder and cover-up events. The plot for a film treatment fairly jumped right off its pages. Then in early April he sent some books about Jane, two new signed copies of his book, and the article in *American Scholar* by Stanford Professor Carnochan about Professor Julius Goebel and something called "the Professor Gilbert Affair" back in 1905.

The event narrated in Carnochan's article was the stunning revelation of the Gilbert sex scandal that we have previously discussed. This had actually spun itself into the deadly web of events that culminated in Jane's murder. The sex scandal was an affair between the married Professor Gilbert, who was a Jordan crony, and a single young lady who worked in the university library. Professor Goebel was going to expose it widely, along with Jordan's efforts to keep it covered up. Jane was incensed on learning of the scandal, and it brought to a head her determination to fire Jordan. Over the weekend that I read that article, the final plot outlines for the film came into a stunning and compelling focus. It seemed obvious to me that Jordan had been trying to keep the lid on Professor Gilbert's sex scandal, but Jane was hearing about it from Professor Goebel and was being pushed to fire Jordan. And of course, evidence suggests that Bertha Berner, who was Jane Stanford's private secretary, was secretly allied with Jordan.

By this time I had been posting information and commentary to several hundred faculty email addresses, including all the Faculty Senate and several whole faculties of departments. One professor from the Psychology Department had been writing encouraging notes for some time, and he had a good take on Jordan and Bertha Berner about which other people were also guessing.

Concerning this, on April 1, 2004, Cutler wrote as follows (with my bracketed insertion):

> Some thoughts: As I may have mentioned, the three female reporters with whom we worked each [independently] were convinced Berner and Jordan had a relationship – how else would she presume to advise him on coverage of JLS death in his memoirs. The newspapers had her having an affair with the butler making her relationships a matter of speculation. She was Mrs. Stanford's personal secretary. She wrote letters, took dictation, undoubtedly sliced open the mail. She certainly can be considered Jordan's informant (and JLS betrayer).

Berner was editing Jordan's autobiography. She was the only one present at both poisonings, and because of that and her many fabrications and dishonesties in her later books, Cutler and I both had concluded she must have been the one who gave Jane the poison on both occasions. (And the evidence for the Berner/Jordan affair is, as Cutler says, convincing. They had even been seen together on a San Francisco cable car.)

The materials I got from Cutler in early April therefore provided some essential keys, especially the information about Professors Goebel and Gilbert at the time of the killing. The affair surrounding those professors tied everything together into a top-class drama: sex, power, big money, murder. I surmised what their roles – and Jordan's – were for the decade or so preceding the murder, and I outlined their roles in the film treatment.

With these elements substantiated and worked out, I was then able to post excerpts from my treatment to the faculty email list that went under the name "Stanford Reconsidered." I began my posting by introducing a note received from a psychology professor:

64

A full professor from the Psychology Department has commented the following: "I have just finished reading Cutler's book cover-to-cover including all the footnotes. Reading between the lines and putting stray facts together, I find myself wondering about the relationship between Jordan and Bertha Berner. There may have been an additional motive at work in what transpired."

Thus the professor of psychology, on his own, came to the same conclusion as the three women reporters. I then rushed to complete a draft of the treatment for copyright registration with the Library of Congress. I also knew very well from my family's history that my great-grandfather Isaac had collapsed while eating lunch at the Pacific Union Club, *two days* after Jane's funeral in California, and that he had first collapsed a few weeks before, after he drank a glass of milk – *nearly the exact time Jane first drank the Poland Water with strychnine* (as a 1905 newspaper account that I had read years ago revealed). I conveyed these facts and again reviewed for Cutler Isaac's known close business associations with Collis Huntington and Leland Stanford. On March 30, Cutler wrote me as follows:

I spent the morning looking for my notes on fur seals but couldn't find them. I can't face that congressional hearing again. At least for now, let's shelve Mills and Jordan. Mills can come in without fur seals – he was huddled all day with executors. Isaac the obvious second victim.

Jordan, according to Cutler, had perjured himself in Congressional hearings for the benefit of Darius Ogden Mills. And, his (Cutler's) assertion that Isaac was "the obvious second victim" had virtually leapt off the page at me and became ever clearer when I started doing my film treatment. Isaac knew all the big players and "ol' boys." He had succeeded Leland Stanford as President of the Central Pacific Railroad and was still its president. He was powerful and influential in California. He was a long-term, loyal friend of Jane's and related to her through marriage. With the verdict coming from the doctors and coroner's court in Hawaii that Jane had been poisoned with Strychnine, but Jordan and Stanford University denying it, he would have been like a dog with a bone in his efforts to get to the truth. Additionally, just as they wanted control of the university, they wanted control of Central Pacific. That's why Dr Cutler added, "Isaac the obvious second victim." He clearly posed a threat and would have to die.

I worked all of this into the treatment and I mailed it to the Library of Congress for copyright registration on April 9, 2004. In the treatment Isaac had figured out that the Jordan crowd was going to murder Jane, and opposed it. Then they tried to murder her with the Poland Water and it failed. That would have pushed Isaac into action. They had to try to kill him too. He was poisoned successfully within a few days of Jane's funeral.

Five days later – on Wednesday, April 14, 2004 – I received the shattering news from Mrs. Cutler. Bob had died suddenly and peacefully on Monday, April 12. My world suddenly became very flat and hollow.

Chapter IV

Cutler Evidence Cracks Jane Stanford Murder
Justice Now for Jane Stanford?

The Stanford University website I came across in 2003 stated that the "most plausible scenario" of Jane Stanford's death was "a natural heart attack." Dr Cutler and I of course knew that the precise cause of death was exactly as determined in the official Hawaii State Inquest verdict that ruled death by strychnine poisoning. The university website was mendacious and fraudulent, and clearly made so knowingly. It was also cloying and unctuous, reflective of some university PR hacks on orders from Peter Sylvester's Office of Development, an exercise in public relations and spin made in response to the things I had told Sylvester in 1983. Besides creating the website, Sylvester had written memos about me and the chief of security had put it about that I was crazy, dangerous and presented a physical threat to members of staff. Palpable desperation in Sylvester and the upper echelons of Stanford was clear, and now after many years of following up Dr Cutler's hundreds of emails and documentation we can say why.

What shifted the Stanford administration and the Office of Development into panic mode after Sylvester's 1983 Memo was not so much Van Dyke's evidence that Jane had been poisoned, but that Darius Ogden Mills was deeply involved. This was new; this was big, and this reached right into the inner-core of the circle of men behind the curtain who really controlled the United States. The massively wealthy, powerful and devious Mills was undoubtedly a member of that circle. We discussed previously how he hurriedly departed New York before the terrible event at the Moana hotel had even taken place that night, and sped 3000 miles across America by train to Stanford.

Critically, the many items of evidence alleged by Van Dyke could only have been able to entail Mills in one way, and that was as the source of bribes. But we now know that there was very much more to it. Bertha Berner, working under orders from David Starr Jordan, poisoned Jane, but the green light for them to proceed would have had to come from an immensely powerful group such as Rockefeller, Roosevelt, Harriman, Mills and, likely, Rothschild in London. These were the men who controlled the United States, and Stanford University was not only significant for the development of their big eugenics program, but of crucial importance in their plans for consolidating their control in the foreseeable future and, indeed, covering up their own dirty business.

Darius Ogden Mills clearly knew Jane was going to be murdered in Hawaii – hence his departure from New York timed to facilitate his arrival in California several days later by the time of her murder. David Starr Jordan was shown by both Dr Cutler and Professor Carnochan to have known Jane's demise was pending. Certainly Mills knew this with Roosevelt poised to announce Reid's appointment as the United States Ambassador to Great Britain shortly after he and Mills arrived. Reid, as we have seen, was Mills' son-in-law, and his ambassadorial appointment was surely well planned in advance. Mills had the wealth and experience "on-site" to organize and execute the plan. No others did. It was assuredly well planned and instigated by Mills from its inception.

Substantial sums of money would be required to silence a great many individuals and leave nothing to chance. Mills' sudden appearance right on cue for Mrs Stanford's death would not arouse any great suspicion (other than possibly in Isaac Requa's mind). He knew all the richest people in California and until he moved to New York was himself the State's richest man. He had ready access to anyone who mattered. He still had massive clout in California plus the financial wherewithal to readily ensure that the police, university trustees, the press, private detectives and anyone else on the periphery were in his pocket and malleable. His power, wealth and influence ensured that Isaac Requa's poisoning at the Pacific Union Club and buying silence would be straightforward. He was a member of the club, along with Isaac and the other power elite. Isaac had known them all for 35 years and had built the Eureka Palisade Railroad with Mills. On moving east, Mills became closely allied to the Rockefeller/Harriman clique in New

York City. They wanted to complete the Southern Pacific takeover of the Central Pacific where Isaac had succeeded Leland Stanford as President in 1894. I found details of this written by Isaac's son Mark (my grandfather) in an item I found in my father's desk in 1974.

Cutler also reported in his emails to me that Darius Ogden Mills was inexplicably then at Stanford, "in town" as he wrote; and that, as the papers reported, he was "huddled with Executors," including Reid, whose real status as an Executor is subject to very serious doubt. All things considered, as now detailed, make it clear that the very rich Mills was the on-site "banker" for the operation and surely the source of funds provided to Trustee Timothy Hopkins, to go with Jordan to Hawaii, where they attempted unsuccessfully to bribe the autopsy doctors to change their cause of death ruling of strychnine poisoning to heart disease, as the Honolulu newspapers reported, and Cutler noted in his timeline.

When a curious libel campaign against me struck up in Honduras in 2009-2010, very similar to the Stanford libels against me detailed in the last chapter, I knew that the whole Utah receivership court frauds had to be centrally tied to Stanford. So I went back to all the Cutler emails and was struck by the "Mills in town" and "huddled with Executors" newspaper comment. Why, Dr Cutler didn't know, but we do now. Now we may conclude that his purpose with the Executors was also to make bribes.

One thing is certain regarding Jane's murder: in 1983 when I met Van Dyke in Hawaii, he could not simply have picked Darius Ogden Mills' name out of thin air to allege as a primary conspirator with David Starr Jordan. Mills supplied Stanford University trustee Hopkins with bribe money to go to Hawaii with Jordan to commence the immediate cover-up, but to their great credit the upstanding Honolulu doctors declined what must have been substantial offers to drop their cast-iron strychnine poisoning diagnosis in favor of 'natural causes'. Did they later conduct their own investigations as to who was providing the money for Hopkins bribes, when their names and reputations were subsequently dragged through the mud? Had information they gained on Mills been passed down to Van Dyke as a 'free-lance' historian? On pondering this, Dr Cutler commented that Van Dyke's interest in the murder could have been piqued by an article in the obscure *Pacific Historian* journal. It was the first to conclude that Jane had been poisoned and her death covered-up, but did not implicate Darius Ogden Mills. The article had been reprinted in the *Pacific Commercial Advertiser* in Honolulu on July 27, 1981 and doubtless went straight onto the Hawaiian grapevine. By whatever means Van Dyke got his information, we can now say with certainty that it was sound. He gave me a valuable lead on Darius Ogden Mills in 1983 and I have investigated and developed it since, but not until Peter Sylvester prompted me to do so after his bizarre and completely false allegations in 1997 that I was "obsessed" with Jane Stanford's murder. That's really the only way Van Dyke would have plucked Mills' name seemingly out of thin air. Mills' money was financing the poisonings and cover-ups behind the scenes.

The primary function of Mills in California with his son-in-law Whitelaw Reid was to cover-up the murder of Jane Stanford by bribing people in order to protect Jordan's place at Stanford. But the greater purpose was to ensure that no traces ever got back to the true perpetrators in the higher echelons of the Anglo-American Establishment on Wall Street and The City, London.

In any case, Stanford learned with Sylvester's Memo of 1983 that Cutler found in university archives and sent me that Van Dyke was claiming evidence for Jordan and Mills having organized the murder of Jane. The only way he would have alleged that from Hawaii was having found evidence there for Mill's bribe money that Timothy Hopkins and Jordan were circulating in Hawaii, with rejected offer to the doctors, and surely to many of the others Van Dyke had evidence on.

So Sylvester and his Office of Development immediately knew – or quickly found out – that in following up Mills and his sudden trip to Stanford with Whitelaw Reid, I could crack the whole case: that whole case being that Rockefeller, Harriman, TR, and Rothschild, were the top of the conspiracy, and that Stanford had been taken over by them under Jordan by 1904 (with "ops" on campus as per Goebel's letter to Jane Stanford in 1904).

Because of the Gilbert Scandal and other matters that Goebel wrote Jane about, Jane was going to fire Jordan, which would have ended their takeover of Stanford and all their eugenics organization plans for Stanford (which were very great), also tied in with laundering political payoffs and bribes as "donations" through eugenics organizations being formed by Jordan and TR Roosevelt.

It would have also nixed Stanford being used as a dumping site to conceal all the incriminating evidence to come for their instigating WW I. The eugenics fronts were their stepping stones for financing and creating the Federal Reserve Bank (that was then used to finance World War I).

Sylvester and the whole line of administrators up to Stanford's President would have been extremely anxious about me developing the Darius Ogden Mills link. That probably only abated when they successfully organized, with racketeers, the Utah Court Frauds of 1993 against me. Sylvester in his 1997 phone call interview clearly evidenced that he had come to know all about those frauds, and the players involved in them.

My fully exposing Mills would have also exposed Whitelaw Reid's role in having been the chosen one (with Mills for bribes) to go do the probate fraud. There is no evidence to be found that Jane Stanford had even met Reid, and no earthly reason that she would have appointed him as an executor. It appears very likely that all the things he did in the probate actions were frauds. Mills was "huddled all day with Executors" and clearly he and Reid were there to force all the Executors to go along with the 'natural death' charade. Hopkins, who was a bona fide Executor (as well as a university Trustee), offered bribes to doctors in Hawaii (with Jordan) to change their cause of death. As Dr Cutler revealed, they refused and reported it to the newspapers.

Mills and Reid were a package from the beginning, with the former running the show. In addition to bribes, they prevailed on the Executors to accept the impossible lie that Stanford labs had analyzed Jane's organs and found no strychnine. When Welton Stanford offered rewards for information on who poisoned his aunt, that very same day the Executors countered the reward saying that Stanford labs had just concluded there was no strychnine. That, as we have seen, was impossible. It was a 'probate fraud' "nine ways to breakfast," as my father used to say.

Whitelaw Reid took the appointment of Ambassadorship on the day before the Hawaii Inquest ruling (since he knew what it would be). That was the last day he could have accepted it, or that it could have been made. It is very unlikely to have transpired after the inquest verdict when he was sitting there claiming to be an Executor of a woman who had just been murdered. With this new-found status, Reid was able to assist Mills in browbeating the executors into doing exactly as they said. Hopkins, of course, was already on-board.

Reid had long been chosen by the Eastern Establishment as the new U. S. Ambassador to Britain, basically in order to liaise with Rothschild about the forthcoming Rothschild/Rockefeller dominated Federal Reserve System. We have seen how he was rushed out to Stanford with his father-in-law, first to do the probate fraud and ensure that Isaac was silenced. Mills, in the background, and Reid were the on-site bosses of the cover-up of Jane's murder, but at the top were Roosevelt, Rockefeller, Harriman and Rothschild. The public announcement of Reid's spectacular appointment as Ambassador to the U.K. was made at that point in time to lend him gravitas.

This is all plain as day now. But Stanford immediately saw in 1983 that I could unravel all of it from just Van Dyke's evidence on Jordan/Mills. So Sylvester and his Office of Development started plotting immediately to bring me down before I could do that, after attaining resources and mining success.

But with the Sylvester Memo of 1983 that Cutler found and gave me in 2001, and Mills being nailed by both Van Dyke and Cutler's tell-tale email on Mills being "huddled with Executors," I was able to unravel it. The reason Mills was "huddled" with those individuals was to ensure that any of them who needed to be bribed to ensure silence, was bribed -all the while conveying them the good wishes of TR, Rockefeller, and the Rothschilds. Such power.

But the primary thing for Mills to do was the engineering and bribing for Isaac Requa to get poisoned at lunch at the Pacific Union Club that his son Mark wrote about and that I read in Utah in 1974. They of course knew I would be upset about this discovery. Stanford, at the top, had assuredly known from 1905 right up to the present that Isaac as well as Jane had been murdered. The university is still run today by the same interests who had been in control of it at least since 1904, and had murdered Jane Stanford and Isaac Requa to preserve their control and to insure that their agenda for Stanford would stay on course.

On learning of the role of Darius Ogden Mills in Hawaii in 1983, without knowing it I became an essential person to "incapacitate" before I could figure out the full scope of his involvement – and that of others in the higher echelons of the Eastern Establishment. That's part one of the essential message that Sylvester broadcast in his internal memorandum of 1983: that I could ascertain who was at the top and expose them and their agenda, that did then become much of what the 20th century was to include, with vast new wars for profit and central banking controlled in their private hands.

This scope of things included the reality that by 1904, as per Professor Julius Goebel, Stanford had been already taken over by that cabal of interests at the top, with their "ops" on campus, who had employed David Starr Jordan to run Stanford for them. Jane Stanford by then was living on borrowed time. One could say that the already taken-over university of 1904 is the entity that had then organized the murder of Jane Stanford in 1905. One could also say that it is that criminal entity that is still in control of Stanford University. That's what Peter Sylvester was most desperate about in 1983, and from then up to 1993 when I encountered the full reality of that criminal entity with their corruption of the Courts and takeover of Banner International.

That was all made clear with the phone interviews by the London film people in 1997, and with regard to the Stanford Police chief. I had become a "danger to the safety" of the university. The destruction of Banner International in 1993 by Utah Court Frauds resulted from that 1983 Memorandum of Peter Sylvester. Without even knowing it my hands were on the jugular of those presently in charge of Stanford University and the so-called New World Order gang that had taken it over in 1904-1905 as a corner stone in its century-long plans for all our futures.

As for Stanford's role in all this relative to myself, I wouldn't know anything for eight years – until I heard from Dr. Cutler in 2001 with the Sylvester Memo he had found concerning me in university archives. I knew the university's darkest secret. I had been informed in Hawaii in 1983 that Jane Stanford had been murdered and at the behest of the university's president, no less – and they knew I knew it. That was true; but, I didn't know that they were concerned about my knowing it until Dr. Cutler appeared in 2001. Indeed, thanks to Dr. Cutler, I found out that they had written and circulated memos about the murder and my being informed about it – and most critically that Darius Ogden Mills was the now easily ascertained bag-man for it, and with the closest of connections in New York City with Rockefeller, TR Roosevelt, Harriman, and others.

Now-a-days the all-too-easily corrupted and/or duped elements in the FBI, in the Mafia-allied securities racketeers, and their socialites have coalesced around absolute necessity of Stanford University (and by Stanford I mean the Stanford as controlled still by the Rockefellers and Rothschilds) to hide all this. By all this I also mean not just to hide the fact of Jane Stanford having been poisoned.

What was really "all" involved was the university having already been taken over by 1904 for all the objectives that included setting up eugenics organizations to establish forced-sterilization programs in what eventually became 27 U.S. states, with 60,000 victims (but with plans for millions), and then to do the same in Nazi Germany, and with the obvious objective also including Whitelaw Reid liaising with Rothschild in London to create the Federal Reserve Bank – and with a major objective to instigate World War I; to be financed by that bank to great obscene profits by these pathologically greedy utterly insane racists; and, then also for Stanford University to become the site for collecting and covering up all the incriminating evidence for the Rothschilds and Rockefellers and all their allied "Secret Elite" in instigating World War I and hugely profiting from it.

It was a vast risk for them all to contemplate: for Van Dyke and then myself (independently) to be ascertaining the first critical role of Darius Ogden Mills in this vast scheme of things to come, with just his first step to be taken for a century of great crimes to come with murdering Jane Stanford and Isaac Requa. These risks for exposure were entailed by their New World Order in 1983 having had to encounter the long-dead past of Darius Ogden Mills that Van Dyke and I had suddenly been clued into. I could then expose all this. I was a marked man, without the slightest recognition of it for several years to come.

The great difficulties Van Dyke was to encounter in Hawaii after 1983, and the far greater difficulties I would face in the Utah Court Frauds of 1993, were the results of my 1983 chat with Peter Sylvester. They were part of the same agenda that had proceeded with Peter Sylvester after 1983. Stanford and Utah were part of the same operation of the NWO, of which Stanford University – the criminal one – had become a cornerstone in 1905.

Now to be seen, with this volume appearing, is what the faculty, alumni, and students at Stanford will do with this knowledge. They are in the midst, and bowels, of a very large covert criminal entity. A suggested first step is the creation of an almost entirely new Board of Trustees (under a restored legitimate Stanford University) with a new senior administration – with no connections whatsoever to be allowed with the Rockefellers and the Rothschilds with their endless wars for profit and not-infrequent assassinations. The legitimate restored Stanford may then proceed to seek all the assets of the Rockefellers and Rothschilds as restitution for their two centuries of Crimes against Humanity with their criminally-contrived wars. The Federal Reserve Bank, needless to say, should be immediately nationalized.

Photocopied excerpts
from
David Starr Jordan's
The Blood of the Nations

Berry states that an "effect of the wars was that the ranks of the small farmers were decimated, while the number of slaves who did not serve in the army multiplied." Thus "*Vir gave place to Homo*," real men to mere human beings.

With the failure of men grew the strength of the mob, and of the emperor, its exponent. "The little finger of Constantine was stronger than the loins of Augustus." At the end "the barbarians settled and peopled the Roman Empire rather than conquered it." "The Roman world would not have yielded to the barbaric, were it not decidedly inferior in force."

There was once a time when the struggles of armies resulted in a survival of the fittest, when the race was indeed to the swift and the battle to the strong. The invention of "villanous gunpowder" has changed all this. Except the kind of warfare called guerilla, the quality of the individual has ceased to be much of a factor. The clown can shoot down the hero, and "doesn't have to look the hero in the face as he does so." The shell destroys the clown and hero alike, and the machine gun mows down whole ranks impartially. There is little play for selection in modern war save what is shown in the process of enlistment.

One of the great books of our new century will be some day written on the selection of men, the screening of human life through the actions of man and the operation of the institutions men have built up. It will be a survey of the stream of social history, its whirls and eddies, rapids and still waters, and the effect of each and all of its conditions on the heredity of men. The survival of the fit and the unfit in all degrees and conditions will be its subject-matter. This book will be written, not roughly and hastily, like the present fragmentary essay, still less will it be a brilliant effort of some analytical imagination.

When such a book is written, we shall know for the first time the real significance of war.

If any war is good, civil war must be best. The virtues of victory and the lessons of defeat would be kept within the nation. This would protect the nation from the temptation to fight for gold or trade. Civil war under proper limitations could remedy this. A time limit could be adopted, as in football, and every device known to the arena could be used to get the good of war and to escape its evils.

Chapter V

No More Excuses for Jordan's Existence at Stanford

The book entitled *The Mysterious Death of Jane Stanford* was a truly historic breakthrough, with Dr Robert Cutler M.D.'s restoration of the criminally-suppressed Hawaii State Inquest verdict that Mrs Stanford's death was due to strychnine poisoning. Dr Cutler's candid and private thoughts on the murder, which were expressed in some of the emails to me between 2001 and 2004, have been published here for the first time. This marks the fruition of his labours, as well as a new fruition for the labours of Jane Stanford. The recognition and restoration of her surpassing accomplishment with Stanford University may now proceed following the complete revelations of her murder and its well organized criminal cover-up.

By 2002, Dr Cutler had firmly concluded that Jane Stanford's murder was engineered by Stanford University President David Starr Jordan who directed the poisoning by Bertha Berner, Mrs Stanford's secretary and his secret paramour. There is no doubt whatsoever that Jordan was deeply involved, but with the dovetailing of our research, and based on the combined knowledge and evidence we shared, it is now also certain that the "paymaster" of the 1905 conspiracy to steal Stanford University was Darius Ogden Mills. Berner poisoned Mrs Stanford on the direction of Jordan, while Jordan was operating under the aegis of Mills. In turn, multi-millionaire banker Mills was financing the conspiracy in close cooperation and agreement with some of the richest and most powerful men in the United States.

Jordan's efforts to produce a fine legacy certainly succeeded with his student, Paul Popenoe, who learned early on one basic of eugenics as written by Jordan: "The pauper is the victim of heredity, but neither Nature nor Society recognizes that as an excuse for his existence." Popenoe was distinguished enough with Jordan's tutelage to write the forced-sterilization law for Nazi Germany and won the personal praise of Hitler for that. His corollary to Jordan's precept was: "The value of execution as a means to maintain the standards of the race cannot be underestimated." To advance this notion in his Applied Eugenics he advocated local neighbourhood execution gas chambers as a means to maintain those "standards of the race." As noted in the *The Horrifying American Roots of Nazi Eugenics*, eighteen solutions were explored in a Carnegie-supported 1911 "Preliminary Report of the Committee of the Eugenic Section of the American Breeder's Association to Study and to Report on the Best Practical Means for Cutting off the Defective Germ-Plasm in the Human Population." Point No. 8 was euthanasia.

The most commonly suggested method of execution in the United States was a "lethal chamber" or public, locally operated gas chambers. In 1918, Popenoe, the Army venereal disease specialist during World War I, co-wrote the widely used textbook, Applied Eugenics, which argued, "From an historical point of view, the first method which presents itself is execution.... Its value in keeping up the standard of the race should not be underestimated." Applied Eugenics also devoted a chapter to "Lethal Selection," which operated "through the destruction of the individual by some adverse feature of the environment, such as excessive cold, or bacteria, or by bodily deficiency."

Jordan's colleague at Stanford, Prof. Eduard Ross, was dismissed by Jane Stanford for public statements such as "the blood being injected into the veins of our people was sub-human"; the newer immigrants were "morally below the races of northern Europe"; and that it would all end in "Race Suicide" was a theme taken up by Theodore Roosevelt.

In 1913 when Roosevelt was covertly being bribed with $100 million to election-rig the 1912 election to ensure Woodrow Wilson being elected to sign the corrupt Federal Reserve Act, he wrote to the Eugenics Record Office (ERO), which he basically controlled with Jordan:

"Society has no business to permit degenerates to reproduce their kind...We have no business to perpetuate citizens of the wrong type."

These writings to the ERO were simultaneous to Rockefeller's "donations" to the ERO of $100 million that was then the substance of the bribe to Roosevelt to election-rig the passage of the Act.

All the fanatical eugenicists and "gangsters" that joined ranks with Jordan to take over Stanford in 1904 (about which Julius Goebel wrote to Jane Stanford) and then to murder Jane Stanford, were truly deranged, quite insane. Stanford is still controlled by these same interests with this same mind-set. Stanford's spinmeister and vice-president of communications, Gordon Earle, states that Jordan's legacy remains a strong one. "When you look at the entirety of President Jordan's career at Stanford, it is clear that he was one of our finest presidents," To Earle and others, nothing short of the Stanford mythology is at stake. He added, Jordan "deserves to be remembered – and memorialized."

Now we all know, however – given the "entirety of Jordan's career" with murders and Nazi eugenics to his credit – just exactly how he became one of "Stanford's finest". He was deeply involved in the murder of the university's co-founder, with the cover-up of that murder, and with the most egregious of further crimes possible. In a court nowadays, even aside from his certain direct implication in the murder, he would get many years behind bars for his obstructions of justice. Professor Carnochan stated: "When you have an institutional story that enshrines David Starr Jordan as a heroic figure and you find out that he seemed to have feet of clay, if not lead, you are bound to wonder whether you have been deluded".

Indeed, many have been deluded, but reading the facts and Timeline here should compel those with the very best interests of Stanford at heart to action. All Stanford-affiliated persons must now come together in a concerted effort to remove from the Stanford campus, and from all Stanford institutions, any ties or relics from Jordan and the unrestrained criminality of interest he represented.

The determination of Darius Ogden Mills as the paymaster for these interests in 1905, and to make these bribes in California and Hawaii to cause the murders of Jane Stanford and Isaac Requa is an historic breakthrough with Cutler's evidence and leads, as combined with those of Stanford Reconsidered. They can result in the downfall of the cabal that is still running Stanford with the PR of such true believers as Peter Sylvester and Gordon Earl.

In memory of the blessed and martyred Jane Stanford, may all persons at Stanford arise to purge the great evil that is in their midst.

Liberate Stanford.
Liberate the nation.
Liberate the world.
Let us all find liberation from the
pathological and fanatical greed of the deceitful.

Calling All Angels!

It's Cracked!

T he payoff has just begun, but we may now state that Dr. Cutler's longed-for success in determining the whole picture underlying Jane Stanford's murder is now at hand. This has been accomplished with Dr. Cutler's leads, many of which are now seen as crucial, but when at first they seemed to be incidental facts of little import. These included, for example, Darius Ogden Mills being present at Stanford with Whitelaw Reid (i.e. "in town," but for what reason Cutler did not know), and with Mills, as reported by newspapers, being "huddled with Executors" shortly after their 3000 mile journey by train to get to Stanford in time to do what they had set themselves out to do regarding Jane Stanford's death. As shown in news reports in 2003, her death appears to have been anticipated beforehand by Jordan, so it was surely anticipated beforehand by others

It appears quite evident that Mills was the "paymaster" for bribes in the Stanford take-over (and with Central Pacific Railroad included), and that he functioned as the paymaster in both California and Hawaii, with bribes having been offered to the autopsy doctors to change their ruling of cause of death. These bribes offered by Trustee Timothy Hopkins with Jordan, surely used Mills' money. He had stayed in California; but the evidence for his money made it to Hawaii, as Van Dyke had reported in 1983, about which Peter Sylvester at Stanford's Office of Development wrote his Memorandum to his fellow Stanford administrators.

Darius Ogden Mills can now be seen as much more than just the paymaster. It is clear now that he was a major cog in the Stanford take-over, and with both the murders and their cover-ups. Especially with his son-in-law, Whitelaw Reid, being an executor, and then appointed U.S. Ambassador to the Court of

St. James the day before the Hawaii State Inquest formal ruling of murder by strychnine poisoning.

Suppressing that verdict, they all knew was coming, would required extra clout, such as Reid could gain by his appointment to the Court of St. James, such as Mills had as the former richest man in California, and such as Roosevelt had as President. The desperation can be seen in the 3000-mile dash by Mills and Reid to Stanford to be with the other Executors, and to have been appointed Ambassador – all before the inquest verdict

The trustees and executors in these circumstances could only be expected to sit on their hands and accept whatever it was that the Jordan/Mills/Reid juggernaut directed them to do, and to swallow all the blatant lies and charades, and mayber even earn some bribes from Mills. Hence Mills was "huddled" with them when he had no legitimate reason to be, except to bribe them and make sure they did what they were told.

Needless to say, this juggernaut of depravity progressed into a fraudulent probate charade. This included giving acceptance to fictional and impossible autopsies alleged by Jordan, even the Stanford labs. The organs of Jane Stanford had been disposed of in Honolulu after having the strychnine extracted from them. They no longer existed and surely the trustees and executors knew this.

Putting all this together can only have been possible with Mills working with the Rothschilds; a search of Mills' ties with the Rothschild give very much to show his long-standing banking connections with them.

Mills had what was most crucially required to make their plan a success. With his well-heeled California connections, he knew how to get things done there, and he had the money to do it. He could bribe whomever was needed, most particularly the staff of the Pacific Union Club where the poisoning of Isaac Requa was essential. As a man of great wealth and also a Pacific Union Club member, he could surely get that done with a few snaps of his fingers.

These conclusions are now quite clear and new facts continue to clarify. In 1983 when I reported the findings at Stanford of Van Dyke in Hawaii about Jordan and Mills being the conspirators in Jane Stanford's poisoning, there was no other public domain evidence of Mills' role as a participant, let alone as a principal, in the murders. At that time Dr. Cutler had not even revived the criminally-suppressed inquest verdict of murder. We can say in light of Stanford's behavior from 1983 to the present that Stanford, among its higher administration, apparently knew about Mills' role in the murder. Stanford's top administration had assuredly known this in 1905 when Jordan had committed his flagrant crimes to suppress the inquest findings. .

Stanford had been taken-over by the "juggernaut" by 1904, as Prof. Julius Goebel's letters to Jane Stanford make quite clear. This already-taken-over Stanford in 1904 was the institutional entity most responsible – still to this day – for the murder of Jane Stanford (and Isaac Requa too)

The great efforts and extremes of adverse actions that Stanford has perpetuated against Banner shareholders and myself since 1993 are a *de facto* proof that Stanford University is still in the hands of the same persons/interests who took it over by 1904 and murdered Jane Stanford and Isaac Requa.

In 1993 they tried the same with me.

Thus there is the issue of Stanford culpability in very serious crimes that in fact have occurred. Another major issue involve the extent of the "cabal" that took over Stanford. Here the focus of interest is very much in the public interest. At issue are the means by which that cabal acts contrary to the law and in violation of the interests of "We the People."

It can only be asserted in this book, and for all Stanford alumni, students, and faculty that this cabal, a primary criminal syndicate in the world, operates with little regard to the law. They do what they think they can get away with, which until now has been almost everything. The events detailed are of the greatest relevance to all US citizens, and to the world, that the cabal must not be allowed to continue: the murders of Jane Stanford and Isaac Requa, the crimes against Banner related shareholders, their Federal Reserve Bank, their wars-for-profit, their assassinations, their psychological war.

Thanks to Dr. Cutler and to Robert Van Dyke the truth may been revealed. The genie cannot be put back in the bottle. Darius Ogden Mills involvement in Jane Stanford's murder was somehow uncovered by Van Dyke in Hawaii and Dr. Cutler set it lose upon the world. The truth in these matters must now be faced – to the very great benefit of "We the People."

All readers of this book now have the information that can assist them to change the world greatly to the benefit of us all.

A veritable miracle now seems to have transpired. To be sure, Stanford University – the taken-over one – will never be the same.

Perhaps the original intended one of Jane Stanford can now arise again. This seems to be the intended miracle in progress to which all readers are invited to join in.

Jane Stanford, around 1904, from the age of 65 until her death at 76, Mrs. Stanford made the University the focus of her life.

Timeline

January 14, 1905 – San Francisco. In her mansion on Nob Hill, Jane Stanford becomes violently sick after drinking mineral water. Tests show the presence of strychnine, brucine and other chemicals indicative of the mineral water having been laced with rodent poison. Spooked after surviving the attempt on her life, Mrs Stanford sails for Japan via Hawaii.

February 28, 1905 – Moana Hotel, Honolulu. After drinking a glass of bicarbonate of soda, Mrs Stanford cries out to her secretary, Bertha Berner, to run for the doctor. She complains of having no control of her body and, "I think I have been poisoned again." Three doctors attend almost immediately, but Mrs Stanford is dead within 25 minutes. Her hands, legs and feet are noted to be distorted in the classical intense, rigid spasm of strychnine poisoning.

March 6-9, 1905 – A Coroners Inquest is held at the Moana Hotel. The jury hears testimony of Bertha Berner and Mrs Stanford's maid, May Hunt, the three physicians, Drs Humphris, Day and Murray who attended Mrs Stanford during the emergency, Drs Shorey and Duncan who performed the toxicological analyses and Dr Wood who performed the autopsy.

March 8, 1905 – President T. Roosevelt appoints Stanford Executor and Trustee Whitelaw Reid as Ambassador to U.K.

March 9, 1905 – The Coroners Jury returns a verdict of murder by person(s) unknown.

March 10, 1905 – Dr. Jordan arrives in Honolulu, accompanied by university trustee Timothy Hopkins, detective Reynolds of the San Francisco Police Department, and Captain Jules Callundan of the Morse Detective Agency. Jordan had already started his plan of disinformation and denial before he departed San Francisco. On arrival he and Hopkins now begin in earnest to suppress the Coroner's Jury murder verdict, start a libel campaign against Hawaii physicians and toxicologists, and bribe a local physician, Dr Waterhouse, who has had no dealings whatsoever with Mrs Stanford, to state that she died from natural causes.

March 15, 1905 – Jordan drafts a statement for the press that after careful consideration of all facts there was no evidence that Mrs. Stanford died of strychnine poisoning (outright fraud), that over-exertion and over-eating led to her demise. He attributes the presence of strychnine in the soda as a pharmacist's error. He instructs Stanford alumnus, Judge Carl Smith, to release the statement after the Stanford party has sailed. He also instructs Smith to release a statement to the Associated Press that Miss Berner had taken the same dose of bicarbonate as Mrs. Stanford and had suffered no ill effects. This fabricated story was later retracted. Finally, in an interview with a reporter he states that Dr. Humphris and the other doctors knew nothing about strychnine poisoning and were deficient othe scientific side.

March 17, 1905 – The four physicians involved in Mrs. Stanford's case issue a rebuttal of Jordan's conclusions, saying no Board of Health would accept Jordan's diagnosis as correct.

March 21, 1905 – Jordan writes Stanford University Board President Samuel Leib to say that if the tonic theory of the strychnine/bicarbonate mixture is not acceptable, the alternative is to suggest that Dr. Humphris invented the diagnosis of strychnine poisoning and put it in the soda *after* Mrs. Stanfords death. Having made a diagnosis of poisoning, he laced the soda with strychnine to bolster his diagnosis. Jordan describes the highly competent and well respected Dr Humphris as a man of "no personal or professional reputation".

March 22, 1905 – Jordan writes a similar letter to Mrs Stanford's attorney in San Francisco, Mountford Wilson, requesting he remind Captain Callundan of Dr. Humphris' actions (in supposedly adding the strychnine after she was dead).

March 23, 1905 – Jordan writes Stanford alumnus Judge Carl Smith that he is certain of his theory about the soda and requests he keep an eye on Humphris and Murray. At the time Smith is a Hawaii legislator. In these three letters and press statement, Jordan has managed to smear Humphris as an ignorant, disreputable and felonious physician.

March 24, 1905 – Funeral and interment of Jane Stanford.

March 29, 1905 – Isaac Requa dies from poisoning after having lunch at the Pacific Union Club in San Francisco. Thallium or arsenic is suspected. It now appears that he had previously been poisoned around the same time as the first attempt on Jane's life in mid-January, but, like Jane, he survived that attempt. Neither of the two events concerning Isaac were attributed to poisoning at the time, irrespective of the onset of symptoms of great disability suggestive of poisoning immediately after food consumption. The first occasion being from drinking a glass of milk provided him while out on business with a client of the bank of which he was President. His sudden collapse on that occasion was reported in the newspapers as resulting from drinking "ice cold milk while overheated on the hot day". This recalls Jordan's initial diagnosis on Jane Stanford as having suffered her demise from over-eating and over-exertion on a picnic on a hot day. The second, and fatal, poisoning of Isaac occurred just two days after Jane's funeral.

March 25 - April 15, 1905 – Jordan exchanges letters with Humphris, Waterhouse, Shorey and Carl Smith concerning his statement to the press that Jane Stanford had not died of strychnine poisoning. Humphris discovers that Waterhouse consulted with Jordan and accuses him of unethical conduct. In April, when the Honolulu doctors are threatening to expose Dr Waterhouse in the medical journals, he gives up his medical practice and sails for Ceylon (presumably with a sizeable fee from Stanford) to set up a rubber tree plantation.

May 25, 1905 – Welton Stanford, Leland Stanfords nephew, places an advertisement in newspapers offering a $1000 reward to find and convict the killer of his aunt, Jane Stanford.

May 26, 1905 – Stanford University officials issue a statement that re-examination of Jane Stanford's organs in their laboratories reveals no evidence of poison, upholding Jordan's conviction of death by natural causes. The organs in which strychnine would concentrate, however, had already been chopped up, boiled and liquefied in Honolulu in order to extract the poison. All that remained had been poured down a morgue drain. Stanford had the heart, but that was an organ which was known not to concentrate strychnine. The executors suggest that no result can come from Welton Stanfords reward as the theory of death by natural causes first advanced by Dr Jordan has been confirmed. The executors concurring with the fictitious re-examination are, of course, closely linked to Jordan.

1905 – Honolulu newspaper, the *Hawaiian Star*, reports that Timothy Hopkins had tried to bribe the Honolulu physicians to drop the diagnosis of strychnine poisoning.

September 18, 1905 – Welton Stanford raises his reward to $2000.

December 27, 1905 – Jordan receives the first of two letters from Jared Smith, head of the Hawaii Agricultural Experiment Station. The letters vilify toxicologist Edmund Shorey, claiming he has given fraudulent testimony in the Stanford case and, later, that he has been dismissed from government service. Smiths charges are all false (most likely having been requested by Jordan).

December 31, 1905 – Jordan is quoted in a newspaper interview and states that the Honolulu physicians and police officials were involved in a conspiracy to extort money from the Stanford estate. Although he later denies this report, it is known that he harbored the conspiracy idea as early as April 1905.

May 18, 1921 – Jordan writes Stanford University president Ray Lyman Wilbur to give him the "simple explanations which the facts permit" about Jane Stanford's death.

As described by Dr. Cutler, Jordan's account "borders on fiction." He describes Dr. Humphris as having been "drugged and dazed," Dr. Shorey, the toxicologist as having been "dismissed for fraudulent reporting," and Elizabeth Richmond, the maid in San Francisco, as "having poisoned the mineral water in a fit of mania." None of these accusations, as Dr. Cutler showed, are correct.

1922 – Jordan publishes his memoirs, *Days of a Man* and claims that "it was Mrs. Stanford's false belief that she had been poisoned that misled the Honolulu physicians." He stated "a panel of physicians at the Cooper Medical College issued a report (the "phantom" so-called Ophüls report) showing Mrs. Stanford had died of a "rupture of the coronary artery."

July 11, 1983 – Peter Sylvester of the Stanford Office of Development sends a memorandum to Robert Freelen, Stanford Vice-President for Public Affairs. The memorandum is copied to a number of files and individuals, including the president of the Stanford Historical Society and the Stanford University Archivist. The memorandum [in Photograph/Document section] summarizes information provided to Sylvester by this writer, Stanford alumnus Stephen H. Requa, who had been informed by Honolulu historian Robert Van Dyke that he possessed documentary evidence showing Jordan's involvement in Jane Stanford's murder. Stanford undertook no reported investigation of record on Van Dyke's claims, but the details of the information provided by Requa were paraphrased and ridiculed on a Stanford website seen by Cutler and Requa much later in 2003.

2001-2004 – Dr. Robert W.P. Cutler, M.D. researches and collaborates extensively with Stephen Requa following Cutler's discovery of the Sylvester Memorandum on Van Dyke and Requa in Stanford Archives. Cutler provides Requa with that memorandum and thereafter all on-going documentation in his research in +300 emails.

July, 2003 – Dr. Cutler publishes *The Mysterious Death of Jane Stanford* (Stanford University Press).

October 2003 – Widespread national newspaper coverage about Dr. Cutler (including comments by Requa) follows a front-page *Los Angeles Times* article on October 10, 2003.

March 30, 2004 – Dr. Cutler writes that an "obvious second victim" in Mrs Stanford's poisoning was Isaac L. Requa, the writer's great-grandfather, who died shortly after Jane Stanford's funeral. Isaac was Stanford-family related and President of the Stanford-originating Central Pacific Railroad from the time of Leland Stanford's death in 1894 until own death – by murder – in 1905. The railroad had 420 locomotives, 8000 freight cars and 1500 miles of track.

April 12, 2004 – Death of Dr. Robert. Cutler.

2009 – Publication of *The Great American Gold Grab* by Stephen Herrick Requa containing a Jane Stanford/Cutler-based chapter, the basis of Chapter III herein.

2010-2016 – Investigations by Stanford Reconsidered, as based on the extensive documentation and leads provided by Dr. Cutler from 2001 until his death in 2004. The on-line articles published in 2010 concluded that, just as stated in the 1983 university memorandum found by Cutler in Archives, David Starr Jordan and Darius Ogden Mills were deeply involved in the murders of Jane Stanford and Isaac Requa. The conspiracy was deemed to have included then U.S. President Theodore Roosevelt and Whitelaw Reid (whom Roosevelt appointed U.S. Ambassador to U.K. the day before the Hawaii Inquest Ruling), E.H. Harriman of the Southern Pacific Railroad (who coveted and then obtained Isaac Requa's Central Pacific Railroad) and John D. Rockefeller, who wished for covert control of Stanford University via Jordan. They were all proponents of eugenics, as essentially founded in U.S. academic circles by David Starr Jordan with backing of Roosevelt, Harriman and Rockefeller. Also included in the scandal's purview was formation of the Federal Reserve System.

Wir stehen nicht allein: "We do not stand alone." Nazi propaganda poster from 1936. The woman is holding a baby and the man is holding a shield inscribed with the title of Nazi Germany's 1933 Law for the Prevention of Hereditarily Diseased Offspring (their compulsory sterilization law). The couple is in front of a map of Germany, surrounded by the flags of nations which had enacted (to the left) or were considering (bottom and to the right) similar legislation.

Scan taken from Robert Proctor, *Racial Hygiene: Medicine under the Nazis* (Cambridge, MA: Harvard University Press), page 96. Originally from *Neues Volk*, March 1, 1936, p.37.

Eugenics Record Office, Cold Spring Harbor, New York

Appendix One

The American Roots of Nazi Eugenics

"Hitler and his henchmen victimized an entire continent and exterminated millions in his quest for a so-called "Master Race." But the concept of a white, blond-haired, blue-eyed master Nordic race didn't originate with Hitler. The idea was created in the United States, and cultivated in California, decades before Hitler came to power. California eugenicists played an important, although little known, role in the American eugenics movement's campaign for ethnic cleansing.

"Eugenics was the racist pseudoscience determined to wipe away all human beings deemed "unfit," preserving only those who conformed to a Nordic stereotype. Elements of the philosophy were enshrined as national policy by forced sterilization and segregation laws, as well as marriage restrictions, enacted in twenty-seven states. In 1909, California became the third state to adopt such laws. Ultimately, eugenics practitioners coercively sterilized some 60,000 Americans, barred the marriage of thousands, forcibly segregated thousands in "colonies," and persecuted untold numbers in ways we are just learning....

"Eugenics would have been so much bizarre parlor talk had it not been for extensive financing by corporate philanthropies, specifically the Carnegie Institution, the Rockefeller Foundation and the Harriman railroad fortune. They were all in league with some of America's most respected scientists hailing from prestigious universities."

by Edwin Black
http://historynewsnetwork.org/article/1796

David Starr Jordan, President of Stanford University, led the way in 1902 in announcing racist/eugenicist "principles" in publishing *Blood of a Nation* in which he stated that, "The pauper is the victim of heredity, but neither Nature nor

Society recognizes that as an excuse for his existence." He could have interchanged (and did many times) several other words for "pauper" that his very own unique evolving vocabulary and "scientific" terminology were producing, such as "the unfit," "degenerates," "the feeble-minded," and those of "inferior stock." Or as Prof. Eduard Ross of Stanford had also been stating it (below) at that time, the "sub-humans," for whom neither he nor Jordan had available from "Nature" or "Society" any "excuses for their existence." Jordan did not disclose, however, how either "Nature" or "Society" actually recognizes "excuses for existence."

Perhaps he just assumed that his readers would assume that he would know how – with him there in his Stanford pulpit, "distinguished" as he was; nor did his "distinguished" intellect "hailing from that prestigious university" disclose to his supplicants what "Nature" or "Science" might actually so recognize (which he indicates somehow they do) as to what any of their available "excuses for existence" might be or have been, and how they would then inform him of their decisions. Was he perhaps implying that he could get some of the answers (at least from "Science") in his Stanford laboratory.

Prof. Eduard A. Ross, allied at Stanford with Jordan, was an early supporter of the "Race Suicide" doctrine, and expressed his hatred of other races in strong and crude language in public speeches. Indeed, he objected to Chinese immigrant labor (on both economic and racial grounds). This position was at odds with the university's founding family, the Stanfords, who had made their fortune in Western rail construction – a major employer of Chinese laborers.

This was too much for Jane Stanford [who fired Ross in 1900]....
One of the most widely read books on the Race Suicide issue was *The Old World in the New*, by Ross. He believed in the conventional myth of Nordic supremacy and the need for a program of positive eugenics in order to preserve Anglo-Saxon Americanism against "pollution" through immigration ... with a chapter showing how "Immigrant Blood" was slowly polluting the purer "American Blood."

Somewhat obsessed with race, Ross was convinced that "the blood being injected into the veins of our people was sub-human"; the newer immigrants were "morally below the races of northern Europe"; and that it all would end in "Race Suicide." Did he determine in his Stanford laboratory, with or without Jordan, which racial samples of blood were "morally below" or above any of the others? In any event, Jane Stanford had Ross, a Jordan protégé, fired for these expressed sentiments in 1900. Today, we can assume that if Ross made these declarations in Germany, for example, he would be arrested – the propagation of eugenics (aka Nazism) there being a crime. But the "old boys" at the time in academia in various places cried foul on "Academic Freedom."

President Theodore Roosevelt ("TR"), an already notorious racist of frequent crude racial epithets, was magnetized by Ross' and Jordan's "Race Suicide" doctrine and generally by their racist fake-science pretensions and pronouncements – and TR made "Race Suicide" into a full-bore Republican political campaign slogan in full-swing by 1903.

Roosevelt continued to correspond about these matters with Ross long after Ross' firing and was already on close terms with Jordan by 1902 (as seen in letters) when Jordan published *Blood of a Nation*. There is a good case to be made that Jordan may have knowingly contrived his eugenicist/racist theories and quite gross "scientific" frauds to pander to Roosevelt's virulent racism. In any case, it was an opportunity for Jordan to pander to and manipulate TR with his virulent racism. Jordan had already been pandering for years to large money interests hostile to Jane Stanford e.g. railroad magnate Collis Huntington, President of Southern Pacific Railroad (with whom both Stanfords had been feuding bitterly and publicly through the 1890s surrounding Central Pacific matters). Since the firing of Professor Ross in 1900, it may be deemed certain that Jordan was evolving contingency plans to avert by any means possible that fate for himself. He thus laid plans, if need be, to eliminate Jane Stanford and to seize full control of the University – while creating the big money and political connections with their combined clout for him to remain immune to any consequences. Feeding the racist fervor of Theodore Roosevelt, to be sure, would be one such obvious means.

Whitelaw Reid was another person of equally essential means for Jordan to insure both the big money and heavy political clout for him to retain his position at Stanford, come what may. As owner/publisher of the *New York Tribune*, the largest U.S. newspaper, and the political "voice" of Roosevelt and the Republican Party, Reid may likely have provided the original contact for Jordan with Roosevelt in New York. Reid was a Stanford University Trustee and, allegedly, an Executor of Jane Stanford's Estate. His father-in-law was Darius Ogden Mills, formerly California's richest man before Mill's daughter married Reid and moved to New York City.

Reid was also, like Roosevelt, a staunch white-supremacist in no uncertain political and rhetorical terms in his newspaper editorials – also warning in "Race Suicide" jargon of the impending "calamity" from an influx, for example, of Puerto Rican "inferior mixed-race blood." The "enemy" he wrote (the Puerto Rican mixed-breed and "half-savages") were at "the gate" ready to "breach the citadel." Thus, when the "necessity" did arise to eliminate Jane Stanford in 1905 before she could fire Jordan (like Ross), this circle of virulent racist opportunists closed ranks.

Both Roosevelt's "Race Suicide" political demagoguery and his personal racist fervor had been structured some years back in 1900 around David Starr Jordan's and Eduard Ross' pseudo-science racist eugenics (that was to morph into the ideology of the Nazis). Moreover, a planned push to enact forced-sterilization and mixed-race marriage bans in 27 states was at stake – starting right then in 1905 – just as Jane was deciding to fire Jordan. Thus Jane had to go.

Most essentially to preserve Jordan's "pulpit," where his and "Nature's" and "Society's" reasons or "recognitions" (or not) for "excuses for existence" could simply be declared and promulgated *ex cathedra* by Jordan for the Foundations with the big money, and then for legislators and legislatures across the country – no questions asked (unless Jordan had gotten fired).

To all the thousands of people still alive today after the crimes detailed here – who were sterilized forcibly under those laws and/or otherwise grossly victimized until the last of these racist laws were repealed in 2003, what can be the "excuses" now given to them:

1) For Jordan's tenure as university President from 1905 onward;

2) For all his racist, dishonest, and country-wide fraudulent financial, professional, and "scientific" representations and deeds while Stanford President;

3) For the large criminal deeds of the Republican President in 1905 and after;

4) Thereafter for the actions of the Republican Party;

5) And, for all their actions and non-actions at Stanford and for the Republican Party, all the way from 1905 to the present (with there being no statutes of limitation on murder).

Without Jordan in his university pulpit pronouncing bogus "scientific" legitimacy for their racist fervors those legislations would likely all have failed. The non-existent and/or fake eugenics data would have accomplished nothing without the bluff of Jordan at Stanford (with the many pretensions and frauds he embodied). Equally calamitously and threatening their Murder Syndicate in 1905, Reid's position as the "voice" of Roosevelt and the Republican Party through his *New York Tribune* would also be in jeopardy. T. Roosevelt could easily tell Reid, Jordan, Mills and all involved what to do. All these matters TR would need to get done through them. Thus, for all these White-Supremacists, and for their Republican Party "eugenics" Legislative Agendas to proceed unrecognized – for the grossest, greatest, and most long-enduring national, political, financial, and scientific data frauds that they were to become, and to preserve their criminal political machine intact through Jordan at Stanford – Jane Stanford had to go. For them all combined, especially with TR on the stump or in the White House, it was easy to do (to murder Jane) and to keep it covered up – until now. Jordan's mistress, Bertha Berner, also Jane Stanford's Secretary, simply gave Jane a half gram of strychnine in Honolulu – and "presto" 65,000 forced sterilizations were kept on track. Jordan's presidency had been saved.

With Jane dead, TR and Jordan could then push the forced-sterilization state laws, which were passed. Thus thousands of "morally deficient" or "feeble minded" women were forcibly sterilized, although Jordan and TR had hoped for millions. Meanwhile, Jordan with his Stanford student protégé Paul Popenoe and with Charles Davenport could form the many eugenicists' organizations which Jordan – with his "elite" level finance lines in New York (thanks to his long-standing Stanford connections to the Harrimans and to Reid), and also currently thanks to Roosevelt – could then raise many millions of dollars for their ambitious alleged eugenics "studies" and "research" via the Harrimans, Carnegies, and Rockefellers. Jordan's personal and scientifically fraudulent solicitudes paid off well. For the twenty years before and after 1913/1914, the total sum was in the many hundreds of millions of dollars!

Where in fact did those many hundreds of millions of dollars in Foundations' funds go? It went for what the Carnegie Institute later in 1939 determined was "worthless" research they had funded for more than 20 years. Some of it went (very unlawfully) into paying lobbyists to push Republican Party bills to enact fraudulently-based eugenics laws in at least 27 states. Where else did it go? To whom? There is much more to account for. Several hundred million dollars did not go for just some Republican Party lobbyists and "worthless" and non-existent data. It assuredly went to, and greatly enriched, certain individuals.

Their scam would continue to pay off for the lifetimes of Jordan and Roosevelt and longer for their henchmen, and was only possible after Jane Stanford's murder. Only Jordan's control of Stanford made it all possible.

Aside from being murderers, Jordan and Roosevelt created the greatest, most costly, most long-enduring, and most criminal scientific, financial, and political frauds in history with incalculable costs in human suffering. That it continues still is shown by a *Los Angeles Times* front page report: http://articles.latimes.com/2012/ian/25/nation/la-na-forced-sterilization-20120126 This the world primarily owes to the U.S. Republican Party – having provided the rationale and the methodologies of Adolf Hitler.

Julius Goebel

Appendix Two

Professor Julius Goebel Proved it All

Editorial Opinion
June 21, 2016

Stanford Reconsidered began its on-line Stanford-based pub-
lications of articles and opinions in 2003 in association with
the late former Stanford Medical School Dean of Faculty Dr.
Robert W.P. Cutler, M.D. on the occasion of the publication by the
Stanford Press of his volume *The Mysterious Death of Jane Stanford*. That volume had one central and simple objective: to restore
the Hawaii State Inquest and Coroner's Jury verdict of the death
of Jane Stanford in February of 1905 by strychnine poisoning. It
was also to show the evidence, with very minimal comment by
Dr. Cutler, on Stanford's then-President David Starr Jordan in as-
siduously covering up and suppressing that verdict while alleging
her death to have been from heart disease. In the process, Jordan
alleged two other completely impossible autopsies on Jane Stanford, one even in Stanford labs that allegedly showed no strychnine in Mrs. Stanford's internal organs (that no longer even existed). Dr. Cutler's book has since become the universally accepted
truth in this matter.

By the time of Dr. Cutler's death, we had mutually concluded,
privately, that Jane Stanford was poisoned by Jane Stanford's Secretary Bertha Berner at the Hotel Moana in Honolulu in a conspiracy with Stanford's President David Starr Jordan. Dr. Cutler
could easily have made many most damning of comments and
conclusions about Jordan's behavior and acts over several years
and most particularly right after Jane Stanford's death. Indeed,
any all-inclusive review now of the timeline Cutler established
for Jordan's well-evidenced actions could hardly avoid identifying many very serious criminal offenses of obstructions of justice

and conspiracy "to pervert the course of justice" as it might be phrased in England.

That Berner and Jordan were responsible was concluded by both Dr Cutler and me, but many other facts were ascertained after Dr Cutler's death which established that both Rockefeller and Rothschild were the ultimate powers behind the murders of Jane Stanford and Isaac Requa.

This conclusion for us re-enforced by our discovery and ascertaining of a $100 million bribe paid to "TR" in 1912 by Rockefeller for "throwing" the 1912 election to Woodrow Wilson by running as a Bull Moose third party candidate. This was so Woodrow Wilson, a puppet of Rockefeller/Rothschild, would be assured as President to sign the Federal Reserve Act in 1913. The $100 million had been paid to the Eugenics Research Office (the ERO) as ostensible donations. Jordan and Roosevelt were the founders and real power behind the ERO, and the $100 million "donations" were then passed on from the organization to Roosevelt as bribes. The possibility that some made its way into the pocket of Woodrow Wilson cannot be discounted. "TR" could not possibly have won the 1912 election. He just established himself as a spoiler to insure the election of Woodrow Wilson to sign, for Rockefeller/Rothschild, the Federal Reserve Act. By this time in 1912, Whitelaw Reid, having finished his assignment to liaise in London with Rothschild in drafting the Federal Reserve Act, dropped dead.

Stanford Reconsidered ascertained all these aspects of the 1905 murders, based on Cutler's evidence and data, but only beginning in 2012. The "clincher" for reaching these conclusions, and now for establishing the final outcome of the Stanford/Requa murders of 1905, was provided by the evidence from Stanford Professor Julius Goebel from 1904 onward. It was his letters to Jane Stanford in 1904 that set her on the path to firing Jordan – which Jordan and the Rockefellers and Rothschilds had to prevent by any means.

The contingency plans to poison Jane Stanford had long been formulated. They were then rushed to get Darius Ogden Mills and Whitelaw Reid to Stanford as quickly as possible to enforce the charade by Jordan et al., that Jane Stanford had died of heart disease. Mills and Reid were necessary to suppress the Hawaii Inquest ruling of murder by strychnine poisoning, hence Reid's Ambassadorial appointment was made just the day before the expected Inquest ruling (and as expected of death by strychnine poisoning). Mills' primary task was then to arrange the poisoning of Isaac Requa during his lunch at the Pacific Union Club two days after Jane Stanford's funeral, while Reid and Jordan browbeat the Trustees and Executors to disregard the Hawaii State inquest ruling of murder by strychnine poisoning.

The final all-inclusive verdict on these 1905 murders can be stated based on the letters of Prof. Julius Goebel to Jane Stanford. In one such letter on June 6, 1904, he wrote: "Events, such as the Gilbert affair, which called for concerted action for the purpose of "whitewashing" one of their members brought the [Jordan] "clique" together still closer.... For there are men at this University who are entirely out of place in an institution like ours. They are kept here, as I know on good authority, solely for the purpose of doing the detestable work of detectives among the students and faculty."

From a contemporary perspective, with that observation in mind, we might conclude that the campus was intensively "under surveillance" for the needs of a Jordan-allied Rockefeller/Rothschild-funded clique with covert and nefarious purposes. Goebel compared this clique to gangs in inner cities. The Jane Stanford murder was in fact a coup with the backing of the U S. President, Roosevelt, and John D. Rockefeller. Perhaps the first coup, a domestic one on Stanford University, by corrupt U.S. Federal power as controlled by Rockefeller, TR, and Rothschild.

Who employed these 1904-1905 "ops" on the Stanford Campus? Assuredly not Jordan on his Stanford academic scale of pay. "TR" Roosevelt? Perhaps. But far more likely the Rothschilds and Rockefeller. What the "ops" on campus were insuring and enforcing was the evident already-established control of Stanford University (through their puppet Jordan) by 1904 by the Rockefeller/Rothschild cabal.

This conclusion is pervasively re-affirmed by the charade at Stanford in 1905 that Jordan performed as evidenced in Dr. Cutler's Timeline after their murder of Jane Stanford. Jordan, with Reid as the suddenly appointed Ambassador to the Court of St. James, could easily browbeat all the Executors and Trustees to sit on their hands and keep their mouths shut while Jordan with Mills and Reid made absurd pronouncements that a 2nd (and then 3rd) autopsy in Stanford labs and elsewhere had found no evidence of strychnine in Jane

Stanford's internal organs. One reason, of course, that they couldn't find any strychnine in them was because Jane Stanford's internal organs no longer existed. They had been consumed, as Dr. Cutler pointed out to us in 2003, in the one-and-only autopsy in Honolulu. For the Jordan/Mills/Reid charade, however, they concluded for the record that Jordan was right: Stanford labs could find no strychnine in Jane Stanford's non-existent internal organs.

If Dr. Cutler had wished to, he could have damned Jordan and Stanford explicitly and conclusively for many of the most serious criminal offenses possible, simply by annotating the events in his Timeline. Had he done so, needless to say, his book would not have been published by the Stanford Press. The Stanford administration would have got the word and stomped on the publication. Instead, Dr. Cutler could make his private conclusions in these matters to us alone in his emails. These included his conclusion, with many others, that Jordan had a relationship with Bertha Berner, and that she was the obvious poisoner of Jane Stanford for Jordan, and that Isaac Requa was "the obvious 2nd victim." Cutler could easily have vented his total contempt for Jordan's evident very serious crimes and for Stanford covering up for them and "worshiping" Jordan. But if he had done so, his book would not have been published and there never would have been front page nationally-syndicated articles about him and his publication by the *Los Angeles Times* and many others, as attached.

By withholding many of his conclusions from his book, Dr Cutler kept his powder dry for very good reasons, but it is those readily reached conclusions about the serious crimes by Jordan to obstruct justice in a murder – and especially in context with the Prof. Goebel's letter to Jane Stanford – that will now make the final verdict on the murders of 1905.

Photographs and Documents

The Stanford family photographed in Paris during a trip abroad around 1877.

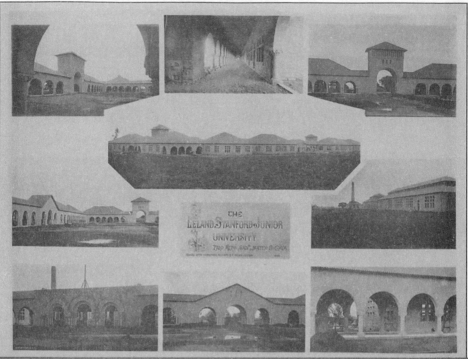

Stanford's First Graduating Class and Famous 1894 Football Team

We present above the first graduating class of Stanford University — the class of 1895. The persons numbered in the photograph are: No. 1, Herbert Hoover; No. 2, W. W. Orcutt, now vice-president of the Union Oil Company; No. 3, P. M. Downing, captain of the football team and at present vice-president and general manager, Pacific Gas and Electric Co.; No. 4, Charles S. Burnell, now Los Angeles County Superior Court Judge; No. 5, Dr. Annie Lyle, practicing physician in San Francisco. This photograph and the one on the left came from Mr. Orcutt's files.

Four of the '94 eleven in the photograph on the right appear in the above group. They are, back row, third from the left, M. H. Kennedy, fullback; second row, third from left, W. W. Orcutt, guard, and at his left, P. M. Downing, guard and captain of team; seated, extreme right, W. M. Harrelson, quarterback.

Left, Stanford's '94 grid team as it appeared in '94, and, right, members of the same team with President Hoover, November 12, 1931.

President Hoover, business manager of the Stanford football team of 1894 and members of the squad on the White House lawn. From left to right, standing, J. Y. Fields, W. C. Hazzard, The President, P. M. Downing, Dr. J. B. Frankenheimer and Herbert Hicks; kneeling, Will Irwin, W. M. Harrelson, M. H. Kennedy and W. W. Orcutt.

Jane and Leland Stanford, Jr., about ten years before his death and twenty years before that of Mrs. Stanford's husband, Senator Leland Stanford. It was left to Jane Stanford, in 1893, to keep open the university she and her husband had founded in their son's name.

Bertha Berner, Jane Stanford's companion.

EXTRA!

The Bulletin.

MRS. STANFORD DIES, POISONED

"I HAVE BEEN POISONED! THIS IS A TERRIBLE DEATH TO DIE"

WERE MRS. STANFORD'S LAST WORDS

HONOLULU, March 1.—Mrs. Jane Lathrop Stanford of San Francisco, widow of United States Senator Leland Stanford, died at 11:40 o'clock last night at the Moana Hotel here. Suspicious circumstances surround the death of Mrs. Stanford. She was taken ill at eleven o'clock, and said:

"I have been poisoned!" Her last words were: "This is a horrible death to die!"

The police are conducting an investigation.

FOUND ON FLOOR OF HOTEL IN HONOLULU. DEATH SOON FOLLOWS | BALFOUR IS | STOESSEL IS

Contemporary news accounts.

The Daily Palo Alto.

Special Edition

Vol. XXVI. STANFORD UNIVERSITY, CAL., WEDNESDAY, MARCH 1, 1905. No. 36.

MRS. STANFORD DIES SUDDENLY IN HAWAII

End Came Unexpectedly to the Widow of the Senator and the Joint Founder of the University Last Night.

Jane Lathrop Stanford, one of the founders of the University, is dead. According to a telegram received this morning by Charles G. Lathrop, Mrs. Stanford passed away suddenly in Honolulu last night. The telegram came from the physician who has been attending Mrs. Stanford during the past few weeks, but beyond the brief warning of Mrs. Stanford's end, it contained no further information as to the cause.

Following is the text of the message received by Mr. Lathrop from Honolulu:

"HONOLULU, March 1.

"Mrs. Stanford died suddenly. DR. HUMPHRIES, Moana Hotel. Honolulu."

Top Left: Dr. Francis Howard Humphris had a room upstairs at the Moana Hotel, and was soon at Jane Stanford's side. Top Right: Dr. Harry Vicars Murray resided at the Moana, and arrived soon after Humphris. Middle Left: Dr. Francis R. Day was called to bring a stomach pump. Middle Right: Dr. Clifford B. Wood performed the autopsy in Hawaii. Bottom Left: Dr. Ernest Coniston Waterhouse consulted with President Jordan giving the opinion that Jane Stanford died of "fatty heart."

David Starr Jordan (1851-1931), was president of Indiana University and the founding president of Stanford University

Darius Ogden Mills (1825 – 1910) founded the Bank of California, and for a time, he was California's wealthiest citizen. Whitelaw Reid was his son-in-law.

Whitelaw Reid (1837 – 1912), after assisting Horace Greeley as editor of the New York Tribune, Reid purchased the paper after Greeley's death in 1872 and controlled it until his own death. In 1892, Reid became the Republican vice presidential nominee with President Benjamin Harrison. They lost to the Democratic ticket of Grover Cleveland and Adlai Stevenson.

ISAAC L. REQUA HAS PASSED AWAY.

Famous Financier Is No More

Isaac Requa and his Comstock Lode partners built the Eureka Palisade Railroad from Palisade to Eureka to service the second major mining boom town of the American West.

Isaac Requa built the great country manor house "The Highlands" after his success at the Comstock Lode. For two generations it was the most distinctive landmark on the San Francisco East Bay skyline. The elite of California politics, banking, railroads, and mining gathered here to plan new ventures and entertain in lavish style.

The Requa family with Isaac and Sarah Requa at center on the steps of their Piedmont Mansion, "The Highlands", surrounded by the families of their son Mark and daughter Amy. Pictured here on Christmas Day of 1900, Isaac had just presented to his son Mark, as a Christmas present, the title to the Eureka Palisades Railroad.

Alice Herrick Stanford was sister of Florence Herrick Requa. She married Josiah Stanford, heir and nephew to Leland Stanford, founder of the Central Pacific Railroad. The Requa and Stanford families routinely moved about from their Piedmont and Warm Springs Estates to those of their relatives.

Mark Requa drives the last spike, fittingly of copper, to complete the construction of his Nevada Northern Railroad to service his new copper mine at Ely, Nevada. The great Ruth Pit was the second of the major copper open-pit mines of the US after Bingham, Utah; together they became Kennecott Copper Company.

Following the completion of the Nevada Northern Railroad, Engine 40 became the only passenger locomotive that covered 125 miles from Ely to the Central Pacific line near Elko. The train could reach over 100 miles per hour.

Mark Requa rides with Herbert Hoover in the presidential limousine on Hoover's arrival in Santa Barbara to visit with Requa (Hoover's campaign manager) at Requa's home in Montecito. In the background is the Santa Barbara Mission.

Lawrence Requa rides in a buckboard with Herbert Hoover to the site of what was to become their Idaho Almaden mercury mine in Wieser, Idaho.

Above: Requa organized during the 1950s the Pioche, Nevada silver lead and zinc mines which became one of the country's ten largest of its kind. *Below:* Mark Requa's great discovery and development of the Ruth Copper Mine at Ely. Massive steam shovels excavated ore from the Ruth Pit, and rail lines spiraled downward as mining expanded and deepened the pit. Eventually, three pits were mined over a six-mile mineral zone. The mile-long Liberty Pit was the largest. Shown above, rail cars are loaded and hauled to the smelter. Over a 70-year history, the mine produced over $1 billion in copper.

Above: Lawrence Requa surrounded with his exploration party on a tributary of the Amazon River whilst on a major gold exploration program organized by major New York financial interests. *Below:* Lawrence K. Requa in his later career as an eminent consulting geologist to major mining companies.

Lawrence and Frances Requa standing on the steps of the Acropolis in Athens, Greece, 1971.

Frances Requa in her retirement home apartment in Salt Lake City, Utah. The picture was taken shortly after the Banner takeover events.

Mark L. Requa II, oldest son of Lawrence, and half brother of Stephen. Mark became TWA Vice President and gold exploration partner with his father and brother Stephen during the 1970s before his untimely death in 1980.

Stephen Requa meets with then-Peruvian President Alberto K. Fujimori at his private suite in the St. Francis Hotel in San Francisco in late November, 1991. They met to discuss Fujimori's and former Peruvian finance minister Carlos Rodriguez-Pastor's interest in obtaining the geological data from the Requa/Herbert Hoover files. With the files, Peruvian gold mining companies intended to develop gold mines throughout Central America.

Above: Phyllis Marie, a long-time partner and great friend to author, Stephen Herrick Requa. Phyllis died of cancer in 2007. *Below:* Stephen Requa on Christmas day in London, 2007, with his new God-son, Paulo.

GER L. BOWERS
Geologist

April 9, 1991

Career Planning and Placement Center
Stanford University
Stanford, California

To Whom It May Concern:

It is with pleasure that I write this letter to commend one
of Stanford University's alumni, Mr. Stephen Herrick Requa. As a
registered professional geologist, I have observed Stephen Requa
develop as both a mining geologist and a businessman for the past
four years.

My first association with Stephen, however, began in high
school where Stephen was known throughout the school as "the
brain" because he maintained a perfect 4.0 grade average and won
a scholarship to Stanford. I also remember Stephen's father, Mr.
Lawrence K. Requa, a well-known and greatly respected geologist.

In 1973, after I completed my BS and MS degrees in geology
at the University of Texas at Arlington, I was hired by Hunt Oil
Company of Dallas, Texas and in 1975 was transferred to Hunt
Energy Corporation which had been formed by Bunker, Herbert, and
Lamar Hunt to become independent of Hunt Oil Company. During the
next twelve years at Hunt Energy, I progressed from staff
geologist, to geothermal operations manager, to manager of the
geothermal department in 1983.

During my tenure at Hunt Energy, I was responsible for many
aspects of the natural resources business that most geologists
never see or experience. Besides running an exploration
department with a multi-million dollar budget, I also became
involved with related projects such as mineral deposits and
ground-water resources. These projects entailed many aspects of
exploration and development beyond the geotechnical: negotiating
with major companies and government agencies, financing and
accounting, contracting and sales agreements, leases and taxes,
and all other business matters.

Next three pages: Roger Bowers' April 9, 1991 letter to the Stanford Placement Service, in which he praises my work on Osceola and Merritt Mountain and concludes that "[b]y effectively applying the modern techniques and by being at the forefront of geological developments in the industry, he has achieved alone as much or more than most mining companies achieve with large staffs. His geological accomplishments have been impressive to say the least."

Stanford University
April 9, 1991
Page 2

Stephen and I became reacquainted at our twentieth high school reunion in 1983. Early in 1987, I decided to go into business for myself as a consultant in minerals and geothermal exploration. Shortly thereafter Stephen called and asked for my assistance.

Stephen had made the personal commitment to carry on his family's legacy to explore for and develop precious-metal deposits. His great grandfather, Isaac L. Requa, was one of the primary developers of the Comstock Lode at Virginia City, Nevada and was later president of the Central Pacific Railroad. His grandfather, Mark L. Requa, developed the copper mines at Ely, Nevada and built the Nevada Northern Railroad. His father, Lawrence K. Requa, developed mines in Nevada, throughout the west, and in Central and South America. Both Stephen's father and grandfather were associates of President Herbert Hoover, and Stephen had inherited the valuable Requa/Hoover files.

In order to proceed in the mining business after the death of his father, Stephen then formed Banner Exploration Company to explore two gold and silver prospects on which his father had started work: Osceola and Merritt Mountain, Nevada. I was immediately impressed with the quantity and quality of geologic work that Stephen had done on these properties. Since then, I have watched Stephen progress as both a geologist and a businessman.

As a geologist, Stephen has done an outstanding job of exploring the two properties. The program, under his direction, has included detailed mapping of the geology, taking thousands of soil and rock samples for analysis and assay, conducting geophysical surveys, trenching and drilling, and evaluating all results and compiling them into a geological model for each property. By effectively applying the modern techniques and by being at the forefront of geological developments in the industry, he has achieved alone as much or more than most mining companies achieve with large staffs. His geological accomplishments have been impressive to say the least.

Stanford University
April 9, 1991
Page 3

It must be noted that Osceola is the site of the largest placer gold deposit in Nevada. Although this deposit had been mined since the late 1800's, the "Mother Lode" source of the placer gold had not been identified. The exploration program Stephen has marshaled and managed has led to the geologic understanding which now indicates this "Mother Lode".

Stephen has built Banner Exploration into a strong mining company that, I believe, is on the verge of major success. His business acumen seems to come naturally and his professionalism is beyond reproach. With his skills and with the assets of the two Nevada properties and the Requa/Hoover files, Stephen and Banner Exploration have gained considerable stature in the mining industry.

As a professional geologist, I am proud to commend and endorse Stephen Herrick Requa. The combination of his intelligence, integrity, and dedication form a rare commodity in today's business world which should allow him to succeed on a grand scale. His knowledge and instincts as a geologist give him the potential to achieve the same greatness in the mining industry as his father, grandfather, and great grandfather.

Sincerely,

Roger L. Bowers

Roger L. Bowers
Registered Professional Geologist

2 / 19 / 1994 .

To whom it may concern,

Gary Heath being duly sworn, deposes and states that:
He is a shareholder of Banner International, and has knowledge
of facts and events essential to this case,and that:
The following will be my best recollections of a Banner
shareholder meeting, sometime May 1993.

The meeting was held at John Ramsey's home. Their were
approximately eight investors present. I was under the impression
that the purpose of this meeting, was to inform us of Banner's
current financial and developmental status. And to discuss the
nature of some serious securities irregularities involving Banner
stocks and the Vancouver stock exchange. What it all means to us,
and what can be done about it. One investor, Don Halley,
(A.K.A. Ashraff) caused serious concern as to the credibility
of Stephen Requa by relating what seemed to me, to be very biased
and second hand information, and innuendo.

At some point a phone call was received from Stephen Requa.
The call was put on a voice box for all to hear. It was very
difficult for me to acquire any real information as to the nature
of events pertaining to the status of Banner, Stephen Requa, and
a pending receivership action. By this time the room seemed to be
full of disgruntled investors. Each with their own agenda. There
was concern for Stephen's mental and physical health. Some just
wanted their money back.I was disgusted at the human propensity
to except a worst case scenario as absolute truth, without
benefit of any hard facts. The phone call ended, in my opinion,
without any real progress having been made, as to what course of
action, if any, that we as investors should now take.

At this point Don Halley (A.K.A. Ashraff) continued his
character assignation of Stephen Requa. Telling tales of mental
incompetence, etc. He stated that the bulk of his information
had come from a ███ ███████████ When asked about the credibility
of ███ █████████, he implied that ███ █████████ is very honest
and can be trusted. He further implied that the only way for this
group of investors to maintain their stock position in Banner,
was to pool our resources, and secure legal counsel, for the
purpose of eliminating Stephen Requa, as a factor pertaining
to all matters concerning the development of Banner.

This approach didn't get very far, because most of us in the
room were not only investors in Banner, but also friends of
Stephen Requa. And as plausible as Ashraff had made the mental
competency question seem at the time, we were not willing,
as a group, to " ATTACK " Stephen.

I speak only for myself, and the things stated in this letter
are the truth, to the best of my recollection.

WITNESS _Linda Kahler_ 2/19/94   GARY HEATH
                                                  Gary Heath
                                                  2/19/94

Gary Heath's affidavit about a meeting on Maui just before the receivership was
entered. I had made a conference call to the gathered Hawaiian group from Salt
Lake City at about the time a street gang was chasing me down at the Capitol
Motel and people were falsifying the Utah State records.

P.02

ROGER L. BOWERS
Geological & Geothermal Consulting

701 Sanford Court
Arlington, Texas 76012
(817) 461-1038

EXHIBIT A-1

February 10, 1989

Mr. Stephen K. Requa
Banner Exploration
P.O. Box 4261
Stanford University, CA 94305

Dear Steve:

I have been reviewing some of the results of field work that was done during 1988 at both Osceola and Merritt Mountain. The data include geochemical analyses (mostly mercury and arsenic from soil samples), contoured maps of the mercury and arsenic values, preliminary field geologic maps, and a written report on Osceola. My initial evaluation of the results is extremely favorable and the following are some of my thoughts and conclusions.

Osceola

John Breitrick recently conducted geochemical sampling surveys of three separate areas at Osceola: Cumberland Gap, Pilot Knob, and Steve's Fault. He collected soil and rock samples and mapped geologic structural features at each area. His results were presented in a series of contoured maps and a written report.

Breitrick found significant arsenic and mercury anomalies at all three areas and in each case the anomalies extended outside of the survey boundaries. This is certainly consistent with previous surveys done by others at the Valley View, North Ridge, Gilded Age, and Pilot Knob Ridge areas which all had open-ended anomalies. I still stand by my statement in my letter of February 29, 1988 in which I suggested that the entire mountain may be a continuous series of ore zones. I dare say that if we could sample the whole ridge, results would show that many of the anomalies we see now will connect with each other.

You and I have suspected for some time that, while the general structure of the mountain is relatively simple, the detailed geologic structure of the mountain is quite complex. Breitrick's work has confirmed this suspicion especially in the Steve's Fault area where he has mapped a complex fault zone that is at least 300 feet wide and more than 1,000 feet long with several cross-cutting and minor faults. The arsenic and mercury anomalies correspond with this fault zone as do higher values of gold (0.09 opt) from random rock samples.

Breitrick also mapped other faults in the Cumberland Gap and Pilot Knob areas. The arsenic and mercury anomalies correlate well with the structures as do higher values of gold. A random sample taken from Cumberland Gap assayed at more than 0.40 opt.

Next two pages: Bowers wrote similar substantiations, especially Breitrick's, on February 10, 1989.

EXHIBIT A-1

Mr. Stephen Requa
February 10, 1989
Page 2

This all adds up to an encouraging picture. While most of
the faults are minor and probably do not have major displace-
ments, that fact is the mountain has been severely "broken up" by
all of these faults through geologic time. As you know, this is
encouraging because all of these faults act as pipelines for
ascending, mineral-bearing, hydrothermal solutions. More faults
= more "plumbing" = more fluids = more gold!

Merritt Mountain

The results of geochemical surveys from Merritt Mountain
also are very positive. Sample grids at the Jupiter and Silver
Bell areas showed anomalies much larger than anticipated. The
anomaly at the breccia pipe at Silver Bell appears to extend
significantly to the northeast.

The breccia pipe at Jupiter is even more exciting. There
the anomaly is open-ended to the west and may extend for several
hundreds of feet. After seeing it in the field, I am even more
impressed with its magnitude. Much work remains to delineate
this huge, prospective area.

All results that I have seen of work done on both Merritt
Mountain and Osceola in 1988 are very exciting and encouraging.
I am convinced that both areas are very large mineral systems.

                          Sincerely,

                          Roger L. Bowers

                          Roger L. Bowers

Note: In this geological memorandum, Bowers refers enthusiastically to much
geological data and survey results which, following his enlistment in the
takeover frauds, he disclaimed, contradicted, and denied. Thus, his original
asssessment acknowledged the obvious gold potential of the claims. Once he
joined the takeover, he denied his own positive assessment (which was based
on indisputable geological data). His only recourse was to remove his *own* evidence, reprinted above.

John Breitrick _____ Consulting Geologist

August 10, 1991

Banner Exploration
Board of Directors
P.O. Box 4261
Stanford, CA 94309

Gentlemen:

As a consulting geologist with eleven years of experience in examining and exploring gold deposits for a variety of clients, I have seen and compared many properties. My professional obligation—and that to my clients—is to provide them with an objective assessment of the likelihood for locating ore bodies on their properties, whether it be favorable or rather unlikely.

Key features are required for the formation of such ore bodies. These include a magmatic and mineral energy source, structures to channel and localize ore-bearing solutions, and a favorable host rock to contain the ore. Additional favorable features for identifying deposits are the presence of other minerals, alteration of local rocks, and the presence of the pathfinder elements such as mercury and arsenic.

The mapping and sampling I have done at Osceola during the past 4 years have demonstrated that all the favorable geologic criteria necessary for the formation of gold deposits are present. These features are particularly favorable in their juxtaposition with the prior mined deposits at Osceola of both rich placer and lode gold.

My professional opinion is that Osceola is very likely to contain several ore bodies along the Pilot Knob Ridge, forming a mineral trend similar to a few other famous Nevada gold belts. Further, the geologic features suggest there could be very high grade vein and breccia pipe ore bodies, replacement gold ore bodies, as well as disseminated gold deposits.

Of the many properties I have worked on, Osceola is my most preferred, and the one that has demonstrated the best and greatest potential for long-term, sustained production, and the likelihood of becoming a world class mining district.

The surface field work has now been completed, with structures and mineralization indicating the locations of the underlying targets to be drilled. For the above reasons as stated in your recent company meetings, I am most eager to see your company proceed with the drilling of these targets.

Sincerely,

John Breitrick
John Breitrick
Consulting Geologist

John Breitrick wrote the above report in August of 1991, showing Banner International's Osceola claim " is my most preferred, and the one that has demonstrated the best and greatest potential for long-term, sustained production, and the likelihood of becoming a world class mining district..

J. PROCHNAU & CO.
CONSULTING MINING GEOLOGISTS

127 Cheney Street
Reno, Nevada 89501
Off (702) 348-1800
Fax (702) 348-1401

November 19, 1991

Mr. Stephen Herrick Requa
President
Banner Exploration
PO Box 4261
Stanford, California 94305

Dear Steve:

I'd like to take this opportunity to thank you once more for including me with the Banner party at the reception and dinner for President Fujimori of Peru Monday evening. As indicated previously I was very flattered tnat you thougnt of me for the occasion and grateful for the honor of meeting the President as well as Carlos Rodriguez-Pastor and the other dignitaries at the affair. The opportunity to meet with your other directors and associates, and informally discuss the Banner gold projects in Nevada in such a pleasant and congenial atmosphere, was also both enjoyable and, I trust, productive.

With respect to Banner's projects I thought it might be useful to pass along a few brief comments based upon my review of information you have been kindly forwarding on a regular basis during the past few years as well as our more detailed discussion earlier today.

In my view, Osceola remains your most advanced project and the one offering the best odds for near term discovery. As indicated earlier, a combination of the following factors, outlined in very general terms, re-inforces this view:

1. The historical placer production in washes draining the Osceola is strong evidence for a significant, nearby bedrock gold source. It's improbable that the gold-bearing fissure veins in basal quartzites, which provided the historical lode production at Osceola, represent that

Next four pages: J. Prochnau's conclusions written on November 29, 1991: "Finally, your efforts of the past couple of field seasons have dramatically improved the technical data base at Osceola and served to clarify targets to the point where your initial drill programs can now be designed with optimum effectiveness."

bedrock source but they do offer support for the strength and potential productivity of an undiscovered source in more receptive rocks on Banner property.

2. The geologic setting at Osceola, pieced together by Banner consultants and yourself, is permissive for bulk tonnage lode gold mineralization and similar to other highly productive mining districts in the eastern Great Basin.

3. The simple fact of Osceola's geographic location in one of the premier gold provinces of the world increases the odds that the unrecognized bedrock source for the placer gold is likely to be a deposit of real significance in modern terms. To put this in better perspective it is important to realize that six districts in Nevada, including Osceola, have had placer gold production in excess of 100,000 ounces and profitable bulk tonnage mines have been discovered and developed on four of them since the mid 1970's. This translates into excellent odds for similar discovery on your essentially unexplored property.

The coincidence of a significant placer gold concentration in a permissive geologic environment is sufficient justification in itself for serious exploration at Osceola. However, I can't emphasize enough that the simple fact of Osceola's physical location in the eastern Great Basin, where the gold discovery rate during the past twenty-five years has been nothing short of phenomenal, greatly increases the odds of success in a traditionally high risk business. Finally, your efforts of the past couple of field seasons have dramatically improved the technical data base at Osceola and served to clarify targets to the point where your initial drill programs can now be designed with optimum effectiveness.

November 20, 1991
Stephen Requa
Page   3

The Merritt Mountain project, with which I'm slightly more familiar
because of past work on adjacent properties, also represents an
excellent exploration opportunity but lacks the past historical
production that so increases the odds at Osceola. This may be due
to the isolation of Merritt and the fact that the northeast corner
of Nevada is relatively unexplored compared to the rest of the
state.   However, as you have frequently pointed out the highly
productive Carlin and Independence (Jerritt) districts lie just to
the south and the remarkable discoveries there during the past
twenty-five years are at least partially a result of the level of
exploration activity. In my view, additional discovery can be
anticipated as more effort moves north beyond the limits of the
currently known districts. In a more specific sense Banner's
program to date has clearly demonstrated that significant
mineralization is associated with the Merritt Mountain intrusive
center. In particular your discovery last summer of high-grade
gold in stockwork-veined intrusives east of Silver Bell re-inforces
that notion and further demonstrates that the Merritt system is
capable of generating gold mineralization of ore grade. What I
personally believe Merritt now needs is a comprehensive synthesis
of past work so that the multiple targets in this very large
alteration/mineralization system can be prioritized prior to the
design and implementation of next year's exploration program.

Finally, as you know I have long been impressed with the potential
value of Banner International's file system and data base which was
compiled through the efforts of Herbert Hoover and the Requa family
over the past 75 years. Steve, in just the last few months there
has been a massive movement of the major, multi-national, mining
groups away from the dollar countries and toward investment in
Latin America with Mexico, Chile and the Central American countries
appearing to be the most popular for the moment. This shift of
emphasis is in part due to "herd instinct" and increasing
restrictions on domestic mining activities but it is principally
a result of the significant change of attitude toward foreign

November 20, 1991
Stephen Requa
Page 4

investment in many Latin American countries. This attitude was
spelled out clearly by President Fujimori the other evening. What
all this means to Banner International is that your data base, as
well as your excellent personal contacts in a number of Latin
American countries, places you in a position of considerable
competitive advantage at the present time. I would strongly advise
that Banner hasten its efforts to formulate and implement a
corporate policy to evaluate this information base so that priority
opportunities can be identified and pursued at earliest
opportunity.

I trust the brief and generalized comments in this letter are
useful and hope I have continuing opportunity to assist Banner with
its various projects. Once more, thank you most sincerely for the
opportunity to join your party at the Fujimori dinner earlier this
week.

Very truly yours,

John Prochnau

JP:cb

From: "philip wunsch" <wunschp@hotmail.com>
To: bihfilesattch2@hotmail.com
Subject: AFFIDAVIT
Date: Sun, 21 Apr 2002 15:20:32 +0100
AFFIDAVIT

21-APRIL,2002

TO WHOM IT MAY CONCERN,

AS A CAREER METAL TRADER OF 30 YEARS AND MANAGING DIRECTOR AND
EXPORTER OF NON-FERROUS AND PRECIOUS METALS (ANGLO-ENELSEA
LTD,262A FULHAM ROAD LONDON SW10 9EL) I WAS CONSIDERING A
SMALL INVESTMENT FOR EXPLORATION OF MERRITT MOUNTAIN NEVADA.
HAVING MET STEVEN REQUA,KNOWING HIS FAMILY BACKGROUND SEEN
GEOLOGICAL REPORTS AND AFFIDAVITS I WAS CONVINCED THAT THIS
WAS AN OPPORTUNITY TO GET INVOLVED AT THE START OF A MAJOR
VENTURE. KNOWING THE RISKS AND EXPENSE OF EXPLORATION I WAS
PLANNING ON TRAVEL TO NEVADA TO SEE FOR MYSELF THE MERRITT
MOUNTAIN OPERATION.

    I WAS ASKED BY STEVEN REQUA AND A DOCUMENTARY PRODUCER MR.
JOHAN ERIKSSON IF I WOULD LIKE TO TAKE PART IN ADDING MY
COMMENTS TO A SHORT DOCUMENTARY CONCERNING REQUA'S PAST
PROBLEMS IN THE U.S.A. AND FUTURE HOPES OF RECLAIMING HIS
FAMILY BUSINESS WHICH WAS RIGHTFULLY HIS. FILMING TOOK PLACE
IN MY COMPANY OFFICE ON FULHAM ROAD LONDON. MY COMMENTS
CONCERNING MR. REQUA WERE VERY FAVORABLE AND OPTIMISIC.

    IN MARCH 2001 I WAS APPROACHED BY MR. JOHAN ERIKSSON AND
SHOWN THE FINISHED REQUA DOCUMENTARY. TO MY SURPRISE I FOUND
THE WORK EXTREMELY NEGATIVE, PAINTING A PICTURE OF MR REQUA AS
A PATHOLOGICAL LIAR AND A CON MAN. WHAT I FOUND UPONREFLECTION
WAS THIS WORK WAS VERY UNBALANCED AS IT DID NOT CONTAIN
ANYTHING POSITIVE. I WAS INFORMED BY MR ERIKSSON THAT MY
POSITIVE COMMENTS WERE EDITED OUT OF THE DOCUMENTARY SO AS NOT
TO CAUSE MY REPUTATION ANY HARM.

    I ASKED MR. ERIKSSON HOW STEVEN REQUA REACTED TO THIS
NEGATIVE EXPOSE AND HE BEGGED ME NOT TO MENTION ANYTHING TO
MR. REQUA BUT GAVE ME STRONG WARNING NOT TO GET FURTHER
INVOLVED IN INVESTING AS I WOULD PROBABLY LOSE MY MONEY. I
FOUND THE FINISHED DOCUMENTARY EXTREMELY BIASED AS ALL
POSITIVE COMMENTS SUCH AS MINE SEEMED TO HAVE BEEN EDITED OUT.

MR.PHILIP WUNSCH
262A FULHAM ROAD
LONDON SW10 9EL

Next two pages: Phil Wunsch, a London metals trader who had expressed interest in possibly investing in the Nevada properties. Johan had filmed him speaking about this possibility before Johan's other agendas began to appear. After he showed Wunsch what he was planning on broadcasting – i.e., that it was to be a smear job on Banner and myself – Johan begged Wunsch not to tell me.

AFFIDAVIT

October 4, 2002

Attached is my prior affidavit of 21 April 2002 regarding my meetings and communications with the documentary filmmaker Johan Eriksson during the making of his "Gold Digger" documentary that was broadcast on Channel 4 on May 7, 2002. My comments for the documentary had comprised a very positive view of Steve Requa and the Merritt Mountain project, the geological information on which I had reviewed. As noted in my prior affidavit, however, my comments were then edited out and never shown in the completed documentary as broadcast.

Earlier, during the making of the documentary in the spring of 2000, and after Johan Eriksson had filmed my intended portion of the documentary, he and Stephen Requa came to my office. At our meeting, we made a call at Steve's request to Mr. Jimmy Nyrehn, a geologist in Nevada whom Stephen had retained for work at Merritt Mountain. I was planning on going to Nevada to see the property and to meet with Mr. Nyrehn to discuss the project pursuant to my investment.

First Steve and then Johan Eriksson spoke with Mr. Nyrehn. When I then spoke with him, I asked his view of the Merritt MOuntain project and my possible investment in it. He replied with a very positive and aggressive view saying the property had very good potential but that substantial work would be required to explore and evaluate it. His comments were consistent with those contained in his attached letter to Stephen Requa that he posted on the Banner website.

I was then quite shocked when I viewed the completed documentary of the "Gold Digger", not only to see all my comments excluded, but also to see Mr. Nyrehn speaking so negatively about the project in a manner that totally contradicted his prior statements to me on the phone and as were contained in his memorandum to Steve that was similar to his commentary to me.

This 4th day of October, 2002:

Philip R. Wunsch

Transcript from John Prochnau Documentary Interview (2002):

000) Prochnau: My name is John Prochnau. I'm a mining engineer/geologist with degrees from the University of Washington in Seattle and McGill University in Montreal, Cadada. I spent the early part of my career with the Selection Trust and Billiton International Metals. With Selection Trust managed the US operation and was responsible for the development and production of the Alligator Ridge Mine. Following a second career with Billiton International Metals in Europe I returned to my home in Nevada where I started a consulting practice and ran a number of ventures over the following 20 years from 1982 onwards. These included operations in the United States and Canada, Latin America, Argentina, Chile, and in many parts of Europe, in the former Soviet Union and in Australia. In 1991 I formed Brancote Holdings one of the first five companies listed on London's Alternative Investment Market when it was formed in 1995 and which was recently sold to Meridian Gold for approximately $300,000,000. I'm currently continuing to be active in the consulting industry and as Chairman of Hidefield PLC another AIM listed company.

056): I met Stephen Requa probably 20 years ago in Nevada when he was starting to work on the Merritt Mountain project in Northern Nevada. He approached me at that time on a general basis to discuss the project and ask me about my views on it. Probably 7 or 8 years after that Steve approached my on a more formal basis to act as a consultant to him on the Merritt Mountain project, on the Osceola project, and on other business activities he was involved with with Banner.

080): Lawrence Requa who was Stephen's father was a very well known mining geologist in Nevada and throughout the world and the third generation of a family of very prominent mining engineers and entrepreneurs that began with the great grandfather who came to California in the Gold Rush and had a very successful career in developing mines there, and following with the grandfather Mark Requa who was an associate and very close friend, business associate, andcampaign manager for Herbert Hoover, another famous American mining engineer who becamePresident of the United States in 1928 to 1932.

105) I met him [Lawrence Requa] a number of times in my early career. Lawrence Requa was one of those patriarchs and gurus of the industry that all young geologists went to when they had questions about projects in Nevada or elsewhere where Mr. Requa had worked. I had several such meetings toward the end of his very long and productive life. By all standards he was both a gentleman and highly respected in his profession with a very excellent record and reputation.

131): I first became aware of Merritt Mountain through Steve's introduction when I met him 20 years ago. Following that meeting several years later I was working in the general area east of Merritt Mountain at a place called Enright Hill with an unrelated party and as a result of that work was re-approached by Steve to consult to him on the adjacent Merritt Mountain project. At that time he engaged me to review the project and write a qualifying report on the project which I did. He also asked me to look at another project Banner was involved with at Osceola that was also located in eastern Nevada. I reviewed that project for Steve and also reported on Osceola for him.

Next three pages: Prochnau, in a 2002 filmed recollection, here contextualizes the significance of that private meeting with Fujimori that he had also attended.

180): Stephen in 1991 was invited through an associate Carlos Rodriguez Pastor who I believe was a former finance minister of Peru to attend a reception for President Fujimori in San Francisco and we attended that reception with Steve and several other associates with Banner at the time. Following the reception there was a private meeting with President Fujimori in his suite in the hotel which was the Saint Francis. We were invited to attend that private meeting. We were introduced to the President and subsequently had a little get together with cocktails with a number of other San Francisco dignitaries.

198): President Fujimori and former finance minister Pastor had expressed interest in the Hoover/Requa Files and the extensive information they included and contained regarding certain properties in Central America. President Fujimori was interested in introducing Steve and Banner to a number of Peruvian companies that were interested in investing in that part of the world and utilising those files as a basis for that.

261): In the early 1990¡'s the [mining] industry in Latin America had been floundering from lack of investment for some time largely because of political systems that were not particularly favourable to foreign investment. In the 1990's with the change in the global scene that followed the fall of the Soviet Union, a number of new regimes came into power in Latin America that included Fujimori in Peru whose policies were more oriented to an open market. So this meant that there was increased interest by the international mining community in investing in countries like Peru and Central American countries that had very great mineral endowment but a lack of investment for some time. THIS OF COURSE MADE STEPHEN REQUA AND BANNER'S POSSESSION OF PROPRIETARY INFORMATION IN THE REQUA/HOOVER FILES OF EXTREME VALUE.

Second Section: Interview with John Prochnau:

000/II) I think Steve's work with Banner at Merritt Mountain on a conceptual basis was excellent. His thoughts about the potential gold and silver targets on the two properties were very good.

030/II) Merritt Mountain, first of all, is in one of the most prolifically gold mineralized regions of the world in Nevada. Nevada has a production of gold of 9 million ounces per year which places it third in the world after South Africa and Australia, very close to Australia. Merritt Mountain itself is located in the north end of a trend of gold deposits that are currently operated by Anglo Gold and produce I believe on the order of three or four hundred thousand ounces of gold per year. The geologic elements at Merritt Mountain are very conducive to gold mineralization themselves and there havebeen a number of showings of gold identified at surface on the property which have never been tested by drilling or other physical methods.

093/II Certainly the geologic elements at Merritt Mountain are very good. With respect to [the nearby] Jerritt Canyon [mine] it is one of Nevada's premier gold deposits operated by Anglo Gold for a number of years. I'm not sure of its current production but for many years it operated on the order of 300 to 350 thousand ounces of gold per year.

187/II) The intersection of structural features like the Banner Thrust and these arcuate faults at Merritt Mountain are frequently the sites of gold mineralization. During my prospecting at Enright Hill to the east in 1989 and 1990 and earlier than that by Borax we discovered gold mineralization in quartz float in talus or material that's been eroded from higher on the mountain from the area of that structural intersection. It's on this basis--the coincidence of gold mineralization in the float boulders from a source that probably relates to those structures--it's on that basis that I feel this is a good prospect. The geologic elements at Merritt Mountain, its location on the north end of the Jerritt Canyon belt, and the discovery of gold there in prospects at the Silver Bell/Gold Stockworks prospects make it an excellent prospect requiring additional work.

399/II) Steve Requa showed me the Requa/Hoover Files. They were stored in his office in the Bay Area. There was a very large room full of filing cabinets and Steve showed me several of these that contained files on various properties that his father has examined in the past. ....These files were documented over a period of years by his father and grandfather and during their venture with Herbert Hoover during the 20's and 30's.... In my view that kind of information is of EXTRAORDINARY INTEREST AND VALUE....I think the real value of those files is that they provide information that's -not available from any other source.

NOTE ON A MEETING WITH PRESIDENT FUJIMORI OF PERU
NOVEMBER 1991

During the period 1990 through 1992 I acted as a mineral consultant and advisor to Banner International, a private, San Francisco-based mining exploration company headed by Stephen Requa. Banner's principal assets at that time were gold exploration projects at Merritt Mountain and Osceola in the prolific Nevada gold province and extensive technical records compiled on mining properties in North and South America during the early part of the century by Herbert Hoover, a renowned mining engineer and President of the United States of America from 1928-1932, and his partners, Mark and Lawrence Requa, grandfather and father of the Banner CEO.

In 1991 the North American mining community was becoming increasingly interested in overseas investment as the old economic and political barriers were removed with the end of the Cold War. This was particularly the case in Latin America where western democratic political models led to privatization of the state businesses, including mining, and other incentives to foreign investment generally. As a result of this situation I encouraged Stephen Requa to capitalize on Banner's exclusive access to proprietary information in the "Hoover-Requa" technical files to identify mining project opportunities in the region. This extraordinary information base gave Banner important competitive advantage in opportunity identification vis a vis even some of the largest mining companies contemplating new investment in Latin America.

Largely because of my interest in the "Hoover-Requa" files Requa contacted me in late 1991 to invite me to join him, and other Banner principals, at a reception for President Alberto Fujimori of Peru in San Francisco. The reception was held at the St. Francis Hotel and included a large number of dignitaries in the San Francisco political and business communities. The reception and dinner itself was a standard affair with a number of welcoming speeches encouraging cooperation in trade and

Next two pages: Prochnau's affidavit.

142

-2-

other matters between Fujimori's new administration in Peru and the United States. Following the reception, however, the entire Banner party received a private invitation, along with other selected dignitaries including, as I recall, Thomas Clausen, Chairman of Bank of America, to meet President Fujimori in his hotel suite.

Accompanied by Mr. Carlos Rodriguez-Pastor, a former Finance Minister in an earlier Peruvian administration, we were introduced briefly to the President although it is my understanding from Requa that he had a rather more detailed conversation with Mr. Fujimori and other Peruvian officials regarding Banner interest in utilization of the "Hoover-Requa" technical files to guide investment of the Peruvian mining sector in Central America.

My involvement with Banner continued for a year or so after the Fujimori meeting although I was largely involved in the Nevada projects and played no part in the company's subsequent work in Latin America.

John Prochnau

16 January 2002

AFFIDAVIT

The undersigned affiant Dan B. McCullar being duly sworn deposes and states:

1. I am a professional geologist, having graduated from Northwestern University in 1975 with a BA in Geology, and from University of Wyoming in 1977 with an MS in Geology. I also hold California Registration as a Geologist (RG 4253) and Certification as an Engineering Geologist (CEG 1862). I have worked as a geologist since 1977, first as an exploration geophysicist for Marathon International Oil Company until 1979, and for Chevron International Petroleum, Inc. until 1985; and thereafter as a geologist and hydrogeologist for Earth Metrics (1986), Engineering Science (1986-1988), Tetra Tech (1988-1991), Bechtel (1991-1996) and for OHM/IT Corporation (1996 to present).

2. I was an original shareholder in Banner International, having first acquired shares in 1987.

3. I have known Stephen Requa since first meeting him in January of 1980 as I was preparing for a two-year transfer with Chevron to Khartoum, Sudan. He was working with his father at the time, exploring for gold in Nevada. I remember his suggesting at the time that when I got back from Africa perhaps I could work with him and his widely esteemed geologist father, Lawrence K. Requa, whom he revered greatly. Steve was very proud of his long family heritage in mining and it was a great source of pride to him. Helping his father discover gold and the secret to the long-sought mother lode at Osceola, Nevada had become his chosen vocation. I felt it was something he was driven to not so much for fame and fortune, but to continue and fulfill the family legacy. He also deeply admired his father for his gentlemanly nature. I know Steve esteemed him above all men and professionally wanted only to measure up to him.

4. I met up with Steve again in 1986 as I started a new career in environmental geology. He told me at that time that his father had died in 1983 and that he had taken up his father's quest. He had been deeply shaken by father's death, and I recall some acrimony between him and his brother Ralph that made it all the more important for him to follow in his father's footsteps. It was his great admiration for his father, grandfather, and great-grandfather and their historical accomplishments in gold, silver, and copper mining history that convinced me to make a modest investment of money and a larger investment of time in Steve's new company. Eventually, I introduced Steve to my family and friends who were also interested in making small investments based on my evaluation of the geologic information on hand. At that time we appreciated that it was speculative, and that the exploration efforts might take years to pay off, if at all.

5. During the course of 1987 to 1993 Steve made regular visits to my house following his field work sojourns in Nevada. Most of the summers he spent in the field and most of the winters he spent raising exploration money and consolidating the prior summer's data. During each visit we poured over maps, air photos, assay data and rock samples. I had taken an ore deposits geology course at the University of Wyoming, and Steve's great enthusiasm, love for geology and economic geology expertise (which I still envy) rekindled my own love for hard rock geology.

6. I learned a great deal about gold exploration geology from Steve who had unquestionably acquired some of his father's great knowledge. I also understood that Steve had studied ore deposits geology under Dr. Charles Park, Jr. at Stanford in the late 1970's and early 1980's. I like to think that Steve may have cemented some of his ideas about the possible nature of the Osceola and Merritt Mountain gold deposits after discussing them with me during our many geology sessions in the kitchen of my house in San Francisco.

7. Steve also kept me well-informed about not only the geology of the properties, but also about the

Next six pages: McCullar's affidavit.

development and organization of his company, Banner International. I had, and still have, great admiration for his ability to organize such a huge effort and remember telling him how much I thought him capable of being a CEO of a major company, and I remain envious of his organizational and managerial capabilities.

8. I was well familiar with the retention of Coopers & Lybrand to conduct an audit of the company in 1992. It was a very exciting time for us, since we were anticipating a major investment and the possibility of our stock having some greatly enhanced value. I remember Steve was working very hard at the time to make sure all the Banner corporate and financial records were in order.

9. I have now read the Verified Complaint entitled Requa vs. PricewaterhouseCoopers and to the best of my knowledge and Belief it truthfully and accurately sets forth the events of which I was aware.

10. I recall Steve in 1993 wondering why the Coopers audit was not proceeding as expected. I also recall perusing some of the financial records and statements since I was naturally curious as to what percentage of the shares I owned and how much funds were on hand and what additional funds were going to be needed to develop one or both properties. Steve was highly conscientious over a long period of time in keeping me well informed and I also received his many company updates that came out once or twice a month.

11. Contrary to a reported statement by Coopers auditors as alleged in the Banner receivership complaint, I have difficulty understanding how there could have possibly been $600,000 unaccounted for. Financial statements had been sent regularly to shareholders, and none of the officers had ever indicated any missing funds. I had talked with the Secretary Treasurer Paul |last name deleted, named Lansky in book| on several occasions and met with him personally at which time he was very optimistic and positive about the future of the company. Furthermore, Steve was always one of the most frugal people I've ever known. He has always lived very modestly, was extremely dedicated to his work, and spent every penny he could find on the exploration effort, the results of which I personally saw both in the field and on maps and assay results.

12. I understand that Banner International Holdings, Ltd. (BIH) now comprises a large majority of the original shareholders and their interests. Following the forced dissolution of Banner International and then of Osceola Gold, I and all the original shareholders can only now view Banner International Holdings, Ltd to be the sole representation of the original Banner International shareholders and the only basis on which we can make the needed recovery for the irreparable damages we have now suffered.

13. It has only been through the facts made clear to us by the International Counsel's findings regarding Coopers and Lybrand in 1999 and 2000, and as stated in the Verified Complaint, and by Steve's gathering of recently uncovered and other suppressed evidence, and by Steve's communicating this to us during the past year that we have been informed enough to take the legal and organizational steps that we are now therefore taking.

14. I, for example, have never heard of the missing $600,000 alleged by the Coopers auditors until this year.

15. I was encouraged to visit both the Osceola and Merritt Mountain properties, and managed to do so. We flew to Salt Lake City first where we spent a day with Steve's mom, Mrs. Frances B. Requa.

145

16. At Osceola, one has to pass by the large historical placer mining area at the base of the mountain that had produced about 250,000 ounces of gold, and it was very easy to see why Osceola has for so long intrigued geologists, especially Steve and his Dad, in search of the goldsource, or "Mother Lode".

17. At Merritt Mountain we visited with one of the claim holders, Margaret Hall, from whom Banner International was leasing some claims. Mrs. Hall put us up for the night in a small trailer house behind her own house in Mountain City. We spent a day collecting soil samples along a recently bulldozed road cut on the claim, and doing reconnaissance on the mountain looking at rock samples, including some very impressive massive jasperoid breccias on the summit.

18. Steve thought this "Jupiter Breccia" as he called it indicated a very possible high-grade "bonanza" type gold deposit some depth below. Steve later did find in 1991 some high grade gold ore samples in "stockworks" on the eastern fringe of this mineral system about a half mile away, and he was moving to expose and drill the gold bearing formation when the Banner receivership was imposed in 1993.

19. The merits of both targets at Osceola and Merritt Mountain are easy for any geologist to see. Merritt Mountain is in the center of one of the largest and most important gold mining districts in the world and also hosts silver and uranium deposits. Many of the trends Steve mapped and sampled in the area, with both his father and later under Banner International, establish Merritt Mountain as being a center of very large geologic hydrothermal mineral activity. Both the trace and precious metals assays Steve gathered identify it as highly prospective for possible gold deposits of large (e.g. "world class") proportion.

20. At Osceola, the fact that so much placer gold was found at the base of the mountain speaks for itself. The geology, to the best of my knowledge, appeared to be right for a major gold deposit to exist. The only question seems to be where exactly, and how deep. Steve's work under Banner from 1987 to 1992 led to the development of a highly feasible geologic model that could easily answer this question, and he was also moving to drill his then-defined Osceola targets in 1993 when the receivership was suddenly imposed.

21. Following the receivership, I lost contact with Steve, and felt obligated to follow the exploration efforts being conducted by the reorganized Osceola Gold Company. I met with Roger Bowers on several occasions to try to protect my family and friend's interests as well as my own. Having seen Steve scared into hiding, and then vanishing, I had no choice but to develop a relationship with Roger Bowers, who seemed to me be very cordial and friendly.

22. I was extremely disappointed, however, at Bower's company's decision not to pursue the exploration targets that Steve had identified and shared with me. I was particularly disappointed when Alta Gold was brought in and drilling efforts were undertaken in areas that I had not understood to be the primary target area. I was also dismayed by the amount of Steve-bashing that was undertaken by Roger Bowers. I have always considered Steve to be a frugal, and highly competent manager, as well as a friend.

23. Roger Bowers had also contradictorily written a letter praising Stephen Requa's geologic expertise and management capabilities for the Stanford Career Planning Center that was sent out to potential investors (attached).

24. Because of my confusion over the events leading to the receivership at the time and because of the personal absence of Steve, I was perhaps subliminally influenced by Bower's attempts to paint Steve as a dangerous lunatic. I never, however, believed Steve to be dangerous. On the contrary, Steve is probably one of the brightest, most brutally honest and gentlemanly people I've ever known. I was extremely happy

when he resurfaced last year and was especially pleased when I heard he had succeeded in retaining International Counsel. I am proud to be a part of his attempt to reestablish the company under his leadership.

25. During my earlier association with Steve, I had the opportunity to see the Requa/Hoover Files that were the core of Banner International's assets. The enormity of the files was staggering. As I observed, the concrete-lined, fire-proof filing cabinets took up an entire wall approximately 20 feet in length or longer. Each drawer was filled with maps and reports of exploration data which I understood had been collected and assembled by his illustrious and esteemed geologist father and other ancestors and by very many geologists and prospectors over 100 years in the American West. I can attest to the fact that it included data collected during Lawrence Requa's and the Hoover family's exploration and mine development years in Central America from the 1940's through the 1960's, as well as volumes of data collected in Nevada.

26. I reviewed many of the geologic reports Steve had found in the files. Each was annotated by his father with hand-written summaries of the importance of each of the locations for future and new exploration strategies. I remember Steve clarifying how these annotated files represented only those deemed of great exploratory value by his father, who had given all those of historical value to the University of Wyoming years before. Steve said that those files deemed of historical value had amounted to about 5 tons of data. The files his father had annotated and saved for Steve were only those his father felt had potentially significant economic value.

27. Based on my recollection of the volume of data in the files, it would not at all have been possible for them to fit into the back of a small pickup truck as apparently recently alleged by Roger Bowers.

28. The events that began occurring in 1992 were nothing short of bizarre. Steve was obviously terror-stricken, calling me to meet him at various locations to listen to tapes of the strangest doings, including a tape that had unexpectedly fallen into his hands and was identified as of a conference call between his Banner corporate attorney and dissident shareholders regarding the illegality of their offering of non-existent Banner stock that had been issued in 1992 without Steve's knowledge or the approval of the company. This tape has recently been recovered by Steve who has again played it for me.

29. I also heard a Banner voice mail tape of a veiled death threat to Steve by someone identifying himself as David Enright who was extremely angry at Steve's pulling the plug on a Vancouver Stock Exchange deal that involved the illegal Banner share offering.

30. Steve has also recently recovered this recording following the International Counsel's investigation and I have listened to it again. He has also again played a voice mail tape I had heard in 1992 of someone identifying herself as ▮▮▮▮▮▮▮ trying to threaten and extort Steve into approving an offering of Banner shares that I understand to have been the illegal one discussed in the conference call tape. …

33. Steve seemed genuinely fearful for his life. I didn't want to believe it was happening, but I do not believe he was in any way delusional. I think he was threatening the plans of some very powerful, big-moneyed interests who wanted the Requa/Hoover Files and would have been more than happy for Stephen to disappear.

34. Contrary to the allegations of Roger Bowers and some of those involved in the Vancouver schemes and the Banner receivership, from all that I have known about Steve over the years, I do no believe he ever made any death threats to anyone as have been alleged. On the contrary, I have consistently heard Steve place his faith in the legal system and vow that those responsible for the evisceration of the Banner assets will be jailed.

35. I lost touch with Steve when he fled the country, not knowing at the time if he was indeed still alive or dead. I was transferred by my company (Bechtel) to San Diego in late 1993, and was actually quite grateful to be leaving the San Francisco that had just been the scene of these prior frightening events.

36. From all that I can gather, based on my recollection of events, it seems likely to me that the shareholders were misled by Bowers and others as to the nature of the takeover and the geology and exploration efforts at Osceola. During the intervening years I enjoyed, at the time, my meetings and discussions with Roger who always sought to be cordial with me, and it is not in my nature to be very suspecting or to want to see anyone hurt. But now I sincerely want to know the truth about how much of the Banner ruination Bowers may be responsible for.

37. In my recollection, the meeting between Margaret Hall and Steve and myself was cordial and extremely pleasant. She was quite an interesting older Nevada prospector lady, and I recall her being very motherly and affectionate with Steve, saying she was counting on him to make them all rich. Frankly, I recall that her evident very close and trusting relationship with Steve lent him added credibility from my perspective. It was obvious both he and his father had had a long relationship with her and her family. I can not understand some reported allegations by Mrs. Hall that seem contradictory to the facts that I know of and observed.

38. During our visit to Salt Lake City, prior to driving to Osceola and Merritt Mountain, we had an opportunity to visit with Steve's mother in her condo. I remember her to be a statuesque and elegant older woman with a great smile and sparkle in her eyes. She spoke glowingly of her husband and of their years in Idaho and Central American mining developments, and she proudly showed me some of the memorabilia from those years of association with the Herbert Hoover family.

39. Mrs. Requa seemed particularly proud of the many decorationsm and improvements throughout her condominium with custom-fit carpentry and in-lay parquet floors that Steve had personaly constructed for her. I very much enjoyed meeting her and hearing about her years in mining with her husband, and we enjoyed a joke she told. Also contrary to some recently reported allegations of Stephen's brother Ralph, Steve and his mother certainly appeared to me to have had a very warm, loving, and devoted relationship in which she took unmistakable and great pride in him, in his personal labors for her, and in his great achievements unfolding with his Banner International.

40. It therefore seems to me that Steve may have incurred the wrath of some very powerful people by interfering with their plans to make some quick money using Banner's assets in stock market schemes on the Vancouver Stock Exchange. After Steve put a stop to that activity, it seems logical to me that the only recourse was for them to discredit him.

41. Any success Roger Bowers and Osceola Gold Company might have had in any discoveries at Osceola and Merritt Mountain after the receivership and their gaining control of Banner's assets and files would have only reestablished Steve's credibility, which may explain why they did nothing productive on the Nevada properties after the receivership.

42. It is not possible to overestimate the damage to Steve that has resulted from the loss of Banner International and its mining properties, and its core asset, the Requa/Hoover Files — as well as of his father's journals, field books, and diaries. Steve also lost all his family heirlooms of great historical value. Steve's personal loss was of his entire life's purpose and meaning, his heritage and his family's legacy. Only someone who has known Steve closely enough to know how much his father and family heritage meant to him could understand the magnitude of the irreparable damage that has been done to him.

43. I can only speak for myself as a shareholder, but I am now extremely angry at the damage that has been done to Steve and to the early Banner International shareholders. I will stake my reputation as a geologist that much of the geologic information contained in the Requa/Hoover Files was of immense value, and I will attest to the great potential of both the Merritt Mountain and Osceola properties to contain economically exploitable precious metals deposits, possibly of enormous value.

44. The obstructions caused by this travesty of events and of the receivership and subsequent dissolution of Banner International and then of Osceola Gold have been extremely costly to all the original Banner International shareholders involved. We lost all the assets we had and the phenomenal potentials they held. These included the vast undeniable opportunities to develop new mines through the use of the Requa/Hoover Files and the application on them of the modern exploration techniques that have been so productive since the early 1970s in finding new gold mines.

45. Indeed, the discovery and development of many mines for Banner International and its shareholders has been forever lost to Stephen personally and to us as shareholders. We, the early investors, are not by and large a wealthy bunch, and we invested in the company because we believe in Steve and shared in his dreams.

On this 1st day of March, 2001, being duly sworn, I state that the above events are true and accurately stated to the best of my knowledge and belief:

Dan B. McCullar

Subscribed and Sworn in London March 1, 2001

AFFIDAVIT

I am a media TV/Documentary/Features/Producer/Director and I have been working closely with Steve Requa for several years on the Hoover/Requa Files project.

Steve Requa disclosed to myself and my brother Andrew Woods when we first started working on this project , his involvement with Detlef ████ and the group associated with him. He told us that he had stayed with Detlef ████ in Mulhouse France and in Germany and that Detlef and others had helped by contributing some funding and that Steve had told them that in due course they would be recompensed their outlay plus a percentage. I asked him if he had mentioned any timescale and he said that he had told them that it would basically take as long as it took to conclude things and that there was no short term guarantee.

The detailed account of the Detlef ████ episode is contained within one of the chapters in Steve Requa's book and we were given a copy of the book to read several years ago.

I was therefore indeed shocked and surprised to discover that Johan Eriksson was stating in his documentary that Steve Requa had told him nothing of the Detlef ████ connection considering the fact that Steve Requa had previously told all of us, others, and Johan the same things and that he had given us all and Johan Eriksson a copy of the same book which contained the same chapter disclosing the same detail relative to the Detlef ████ situation.

Signed:

Paul W Woods 10|12|02.

Paul W Woods
Producer/Director

Wood's affidavit.

AFFIDAVIT

The undersigned affiant Joanne Weiss, being duly sworn, deposes and states:

1. I am a practicing therapist with many years' experience and I invested in Banner International in October of 1988. My hope was that the investment would pay off within a few years. I knew it was a risk investment but did so because my friend Dennis Miller had been working with Steve Requa on a promotional film for the company. Dennis believed strongly in the project and after meeting Steve Requa myself and discussing the potential of the mining properties, I followed Dennis' advice and invested in Banner Exploration.

2. My impression of Steve Requa at that time was that he was honest, sincere, had a deep knowledge of mining development and exploration and was utterly dedicated to bringing in a producing gold mine.

3. From that time onwards I received continuos company updates appraising me of the company's progress and felt that serious plans were being executed with good judgement and careful financial management also had confirmation of the exploration progress since my son accompanied Dennis Miller and Steve Requa on one of his film shoots to the Osceola property.

4. Following the imposition of the receivership, Steve Requa came to my home in September 1993. He talked about ruthless interests who were taking over Banner International and death threats that were being made against him. He was terror-stricken and obviously genuinely afraid.

5.   The next information I received was a letter from Roger Bowers saying that after Banner Exploration had been placed in receivership that a new company, called Osceola Gold Mining Company, had been formed and taken over Banner's assets. In subsequent communication from Bowers I was told

Next three pages: Weiss affidavit.

that I had to exchange my original Banner Exploration shares
for shares in the newly formed company or they would become
worthless. I eventually agreed to do this, since there was
no word from Steve at that time and we did not know where he
was. I later heard that he had fled to England.

6. Since transferring my shares to Osceola Gold Mining
Company, all the information I have received from that
organization has been about the total dissolution of that
corporate entity and its winding up in bankruptcy. This, of
course, rendered my original investment in Banner
Exploration worthless.

7. It is only during the past year when I received the
information provided by Steve and his legal representative,
that I learned of the complaint against Coopers and the
reasons for taking action against them. I had had no
knowledge that Coopers' auditors had claimed a $600,000
deficit in the company accounts. This claim is particularly
surprising to me since I have always observed Steve to be
scrupulously careful and honest in his money management.

8. The only other thing I can add is that I spoke to
Bowers on several occasions to try and find out what was
happening to my investment. Bowers said that the principals
of the company were afraid that Steve would take some
violent action against them. I felt that this was a
deliberate effort to discredit Steve. As a therapist and
having known Steve for some time, I did not believe he was a
threat to anyone. I understand from Steve that many such
allegations were made against him by those who got control
of Banner's assets, and I do not think they are believable.

9. I, like a majority of BI shareholders, have accordingly
assigned to Banner International Holdings, Ltd. (BIH) my
rights to litigate and recover Banner International (BI)
assets and compensation for the damages in consideration for
my taking BIH shares. I have the same number of shares in

BIH as I did in BI, and the structure of BIH is the same as
BI. For the on-going purposes of the original shareholders,
BIH is the re-organized corporate body of BI.

10. BIH is therefore the only entity in existence to
represent us original BI shareholders in the recoveries for
our losses. I continue to trust Stephen Requa and the re-
organized BIH, and this is now our only vehicle for justice
and recompense.

This 2 day of April, 2001:

------------------ Joanne Weiss

----------------------- Witness   Date

State of _California_

County of _Marin_   } ss.

Subscribed and sworn to (or affirmed) before me
this 2²ᵈ day of April 2001, by
(1) Joanne Mae Weiss
                              Name of Signer(s)
(2) _____
                              Name of Signer(s)

MARTHA ROMERO
COMM. #1292375
NOTARY PUBLIC-CALIFORNIA
MARIN COUNTY
My Comm. Expires February 24, 2008

_____
Signature of Notary Public

153